YOUR MONEY OR YOUR LIFE!

UNMASK THE HIGHWAY ROBBERS

–

ENJOY WEALTH IN EVERY AREA OF YOUR LIFE

STEVE CONLEY

mPowr

First Published in Great Britain 2019 by mPowr (Publishing) Limited

www.mpowrpublishing.com

A catalogue record for this book is available from the British Library
ISBN – 978-1-907282-77-5

Design by Martyn Pentecost
mPowr Publishing 'Clumpy™' Logo by e-nimation.com
Clumpy™ and the Clumpy™ Logo are trademarks of mPowr Limited

The mPowr Legacy

Every moment of your life has the potential to be more than every moment of your life. As you invest each day into something greater than yourself—lasting longer than your lifetime, influencing those yet to be born—you create a legacy. A legacy that serves others beyond the minutes, hours and years you will ever spend on Earth. The mPowr Publishing mission is to inspire your legacy—to help you create it through the books and media you develop. Every title we publish is more than the sum of its parts, with deeper impact, broader transformation and, at its heart, a legacy that is yours in this moment, right now.

FOR
MUM AND DAD

CONTENTS

I'M BALANCE

You enjoy a bargain, don't you?

From that must-have item reduced in the sales, to the three-for-two on your weekly groceries, we all get that warm and fuzzy feeling when we bag an amazing offer. It is built into us—a little shot of dopamine that lets us know we did good.

Do you ever stop and think about the business that manufactures those products?

Ever wonder how the 70% reduction will affect their turnover? Can they pay their staff a Christmas bonus if you favour the BOGOF (buy one, get one free) over a full-price purchase? Will that larger warehouse space be affordable for them if you use that time-sensitive discount code?

Why on earth would you? As the consumer, any suggestion that you ponder the well-being of anyone other than yourself usually sparks utter consternation.

If you, like most people, are thinking the money is better off in your pocket instead of anybody else's, congratulations! You have just identified how the financial services industry views you.

Yes, you!

As a commodity that solely benefits them.

They do not care if you work hard for a living, if you have bills to pay or dreams to fulfil. They barely see you as a person and certainly not as their client. Your money is their client!

The suggestion that a bank cares about you over their own agenda provokes the same sense of utter bemusement in them as you felt a moment ago.

No.

Banks care about money and therefore focus on the 5% of people with money, not the underserved, not the 95% of their clientele. And that sensation you experience when you snag a bargain is exactly what banking organisations crave for themselves.

They hunger for that profit at your expense. Slathering at the thought of your empty purse and wallet bereft.

Now, this is not news—banks have been painted as the *bad guys* for decades. We already have that niggling mental image of the crafty cutpurse or shadowy highwayman when it comes to the ethics and tactics of banks.

However, these are not lone muggers that skulk down narrow passageways; they were never the solitary pickpocket that risks everything with a swipe of their fingers. Banks are huge, pan-global businesses that keep governments in strangleholds and the media in a spell-like trance of erotic proportions!

At the very core of their strategy is one simple and rather daunting fact:

You are never truly in control of your own life.

You need money to survive, which means you must *work for a living* (as many a parent has uttered with consternation to their bewildered child). So you spend your entire life working to see most of your hard-earned cash spent on that aforementioned living.

However, you are alive. You are *living* already! You do not need to *earn a living*—you are achieving that particular wonder every single day of your life. The ambiguity formed by confusing being alive (living) with making money to pay for our needs (what we refer to as *earning a living*) blinds us to a long-perpetrated myth…

You do not need to earn a living—living is already yours to possess in this moment. Yet, you do need to fulfil your needs. You have wants and needs, but these are only important to the financial services industry when they can leverage those wants and needs against you.

When your fundamental needs are not being met, your primal brain goes haywire and you enter a state of high alert until those needs are satiated. A bank, for example, will play on those emotions to provoke a certain behaviour, which usually revolves around signing up for their product or service.

Signing up for their solution, no matter how disconnected from the actual problem, helps alleviate the stress.

Every person, regardless of who they are, has a set of fundamental needs.

From the gleaming towers of Canary Wharf to the slums of Orangi Town, regardless of gender and gender identity, ethnicity or cultural heritage, sexual orientation or religious beliefs, we cannot survive or thrive unless these needs are met.

When all the essential needs are met, we experience a shift from survival mode to a state of self-actualisation. Here, we feel an overwhelming urge to realise who we are as individuals—what makes us unique. We tap into a deep yearning to be aligned with who we truly are.

To be complete, whole and happy we must fulfil both needs. The need to survive and the need to self-actualise. When people are not all they want to be in the world they feel pain. The pain of lacking the necessities or the pain of not living their truth.

This divides us into three distinct categories.

1. Those who have discovered a balance between having everything they need to survive and living their truth (self-actualisation).

2. The people who have achieved their basic needs yet fail to push themselves further—to seek and live their truth. So, the pain they feel (from living a disingenuous life) triggers a need to mask the pain. This usually results in them seeking out more of their basic needs. More food, more relationships and more money. Bigger houses, faster cars, better substances. They fall back on what they know and strive to fill the void with *more*, instead of adapting to their truth.

3. Finally, there are people who know their truth and seek to actualise it without the necessary foundations in place. They live their truth, whilst existing on the verge of homelessness, starvation or intense loneliness.

People who live in a perpetual state of being out-of-balance portray an outside appearance of fulfilment, whilst within they are utterly shattered; feeling bereft, not holding it together, not wanting to be here.

When imbalanced, people plan their finances based on what they want to project to meet the expectations of other people; neglecting their inner emotional needs and values. Or they pursue emotional needs and values without having the basics needed for long-term survival.

Either way, they do so at their peril.

Best-laid plans are laid to waste—financial security as an intellectual and practical veneer that hides a distinct lack of compassion and belonging. Whilst the appearance of altruism and wisdom masks a person who can barely make ends meet.

Most people do not have a plan which has been created by them. Without a plan for yourself you will inexorably be bound by someone else's.

Their plan is that you spend almost all of your life working hard on *making a living*, whilst gambling you can use the remainder of your life (retirement) to buy freedom in old age. Many lose that bet. With each passing generation, the number of losers is getting higher.

The standard plan offered to an unprepared audience usually follows a set model— accumulate, crystallise, *decumulate* (de-accumulation), succession, protection.

In Britain, 42% of marriages end in divorce, over half of them in the first ten years. The number one reason is infidelity. The second is money. Different spending habits, different financial goals and different values lead to a power struggle.

One in five families in the UK are cohabiting couples, where separation rates are five times that of married couples. One in two cohabiting couples think they have common-law marriage rights. They do not.

Divorce or separation can destroy many a well-made financial plan.

Plans need solid foundations—they must satisfy both on the outside and on the inside for you to feel complete, whole and safe. Disconnected plans are constructed on shifting sand and are all too often doomed to fail.

Conversely, some people experience ease and grace on the inside, while outside they struggle with the world. These individuals, who easily express their emotional needs and values, neglect their finances and the practicalities of everyday life. Such arrangements are also doomed to fail.

Inner and outer world conflict also happens when you live as others expect you to live and are not true to yourself. People compromise on their values when they adopt the values of other people. Their beliefs become conditioned.

Conditioned beliefs are ingrained through mainstream media, religion, society, parents, families, teachers and those in power (big corporate bosses, economists and policymakers).

People are faced with doubts, fears, struggles, blockages, manipulations and control. The limited view, the version of the world they adopt through the framework of the values of others, is so deeply ingrained, people believe in it without question.

The truth is, prosperity manifests for those whose values we live by.

What are your values?

Do you truly live by them?

Have you ever found yourself living as others expect you to live?

Living to their values and not your own?

To the world you are prosperous yet inwardly you feel incomplete, underappreciated and compromised in some way?

What would it take for you to leave behind the rules imposed by others?

Conversely, you may live to your own rules, but do you find the daily essentials such as earning enough money a complete mystery?

Do you feel the hunger of poverty as you feed the hunger of life purpose?

How many years of loneliness have you endured to follow your path, at the expense of companionship?

Your values define you.

Your values are what you judge to be important in life. For yourself. For others. For the planet. Values matter.

Values are essential for us—to hold our thoughts, feelings and actions together. Values give us a sense of direction; they give our lives meaning and purpose. If you do not live to your own values, you will automatically live to the values of someone else.

or Your Life

If you feel out of control; bound by the values of others, this book is here to help you. I am here to help you.

Here you will discover how to cash in on your dreams. How to live an inspired life whilst maintaining a healthy bank balance. How to achieve financial freedom. How to create your own set of rules.

And the importance of this cannot be truly grasped, because your value cannot be quantified—not through a period of time or an amount of money. Whilst you will be told over and over again that you are only worth the wage you earn, you can never be paid enough to truly reflect what you are worth.

You may only have one fleeting, precious lifetime to live. However, the effects of that lifetime cannot be limited by the number of years you live. Most live a life far shorter in impact upon the planet than their years on it, whilst the reach and influence of others extends for centuries.

This book will release you from a life lived in fear of money or a slave to it. A life where money is viewed as a barrier to fulfilling your dreams—or as more important than your dreams.

You will uncover how to remain calm and confident around money. How to attract money by taking practical steps. How you will build your dream life with the financial architecture in place to support it.

How to make money work for you and how you fill your lifetime to extend your reach beyond what you think is possible.

These pages possess the secrets of money mastery—the master key to unlock vaults of opportunity in very real terms.

I will share with you the combination to safe-locked secrets—*the secrets banks do not want you to know.*

Through my career with the top UK banks, I learnt how far these banks would go to keep their secrets—their hold over you and your life. I also discovered how you can achieve freedom from the chains you did not even know you were tangled in.

This is what the banking industry does—they engineer a world where your failure is their success… Where you are teased, rewarded or beaten with a stick towards a specific mindset. This mindset causes you to think, act and behave in ways that make bankers wealthier.

As the customer of your bank, you feel you have value, entitlements and rights. You believe you deserve a high degree of service, security and care. You hope your bank sees you as a great customer, who they want to keep and reward.

You are not a customer of your bank. Your money is.

The bank calculates your lifetime value to them, measured by your contribution to their profits. Rich or poor, you have a significant profit contribution to the bank over your lifetime.

Hidden fees on your lifetime savings will contribute to this, what contributes more will be your future lifetime debt (secured and unsecured) and the extortionate fees they extract from your aberrant behaviour.

People use unsecured debt over a lifetime to fund major purchases, this habitual behaviour contributes significantly to bank coffers.

You may think interest rates levied by payday lenders are high, check out the fees deducted on overdrafts of so-called *free* banking. These are far higher. Many people live from payday to overdraft in each pay cycle.

Banks use terms such as *front of wallet,* when driving you to use your credit card to pay for goods. *Share of wallet,* as they seek to deepen the product relationship with you. *Cross-sell* and *Upsell*, when the more products you own, the stickier your relationship is with the bank (when they know they can up their fees without losing you as a customer).

The bank does not want you to become good at managing your money. For example, habitually clearing your credit card balance before incurring charges will adversely impact your credit rating. Being good at managing your money detrimentally impacts your lifetime worth to the bank!

And the banks will mislead, bully and harass to stop you from understanding the impact of this upon you. This is not only unethical, it is also endemic to every aspect of society. As holders of the purse strings, banks will consistently act to negate any competition to their financial domination of your life.

What matters most to customers matters least to the banks. It is no wonder so many people do not trust banks—nor should they. Year after year, the financial services industry is the least trusted of all industries globally in every market[1].

This stark reality is even more tragic. For when bank customers were asked what mattered most, they said *trust*. Paradoxically, what mattered most to customers, mattered least to the banks.

Bankers have issues with trust, because bankers have lying issues.

Trust is vital when it comes to financial advice and financial decisions. So, before we explore those all-important secrets the banks cherish so greedily, permit me to share with you how I came to be in the position to know these secrets, why they are so important to you, and what qualifies me to reveal them to you.

In my financial industry career, I have been six-times market leader. Six-times world champion of the banking world. I created six market firsts, won multiple awards—best product in Britain, best product in the world and so on.

One of these financial products saved the lives of five million children and the first client was the pope.

Through all this, there are two industry firsts that disrupted the markets to their very core. The first was the life and pension industry, which had the reputation for being antiquated, fuddy-duddy, dusty places that took months to turn around requests for statements, continually blaming backlogs and restricting trades to one switch a year.

In 2003 I brought platforms to the UK from Australia and US. Instantly, you could get valuations and switch 24/7 on your desktop. The life and pension industry had to change overnight or die. They changed.

Two years later I achieved the same in the fund management industry. Though I did not make life easy for myself!

I had left the big companies, offering me eye-watering incentives to build them *me too* platforms. No, I was on my next mission—saving the UK's fourth largest IFA (Independent Financial Advisor) network from collapse.

A by-product of this mission was to create something that fundamentally disrupted the fund management industry…

My task was to shift £7 billion of assets to the UK's first intermediary platform under a fantastic investment proposition. The challenge was, retail investment propositions were not that great, because the fund management industry reserved their best stuff for private clients and institutions.

Banks call this change, *democratisation*.

My aim was to take what exclusive clients were getting and make it available to everybody. Until that point the public only had access to underperforming *closet trackers* stuffed with charges. If you do not know what these are, do not panic! Most people didn't either—they still do not—but take my word, there were bad! Really bad!

In 2005, we launched *Tactica*. Managed by Goldman Sachs, this was the first retail multi-asset fund as we know them today. All fund houses the length of Cannon Street and beyond had to follow suit to ensure their survival.

My endeavours were supported by one of the scariest people in the City! Seven-foot tall, give or take an inch, he petrified politicians half to death and was reputed to keep piranha in his Mayfair office!

I asked him for financial backing to save the firm, which he agreed to do. When asked why he said yes, he explained *"No one has ever had the balls to ask me before!"*

The deal to save the firm failed due to complications, just before completion. This left me with just twenty-four hours to sell the business or risk twelve hundred advisers losing their livelihood.

I signed the papers whilst on honeymoon. Handing the phone back to the waiter I found myself in the unenviable situation of turning to my new wife (and project manager) and firing her from her job.

Today, four out of five people use these platforms or retail multi-asset funds to invest.

When an industry or institution is built upon a philosophy of money is the client, those with the greatest share of money are going to be the most treasured. It takes a different set of values to change a ground-in, habitual strategy. It takes a different set of values and tenacity, the likes of which can only flow from the very core of your being.

December 2011, I sat at a grey table in a small glass-walled meeting room in one of the gleaming towers that dominate Canary Wharf, London.

On the table were two, litre glass bottles of water—one sparkling, one still, emblazoned with the HSBC branding. As I waited, I, like the water, tilted with the slight sway of the tower as it moved gently in the wind. The room was heavy with low expectations.

After conducting successful financial planning pilot programmes for HSBC, the feedback was astounding. Higher share of wallet. Higher conversion. Bigger case size. Lower conduct risk. Plus, clients said it was the best financial conversation in their life.

Armed with this exceptional feedback and data, I proposed that we roll out the scheme for the benefit of 500 million customers globally (much in the same way I had done with earlier projects). For me this was a simple decision—a win/win for the banks and their customers.

The door opened and a familiar colleague strode into the office. In his mid-forties, he was tall, with short black hair, pale complexion, pointed featured and beady-eyed. His smart, dark suit, white shirt, bright red tie, presented the illusion of confidence, though he said little. He seldom did.

Placing a smart black leather folder on the table, he reached for the still water as he took his seat. "The board have rejected the proposal," he said, matter of factly. "We're going to do what Barclays has done, we are going to lay off the advisers."

I was speechless.

Dumbstruck at the thought of it, a chill ran down my spine.

It was unexpected. It was devastating. Not just for me, but for the thousands of advisers who would lose their jobs, their vocations and experience terrible pain in their disrupted families. My hand trembled as I reached for the water to pour myself a glass.

"The decision was unanimous," he continued. "Wealth has proved a zero-sum game for the banks for decades. Unless the client invests £500,000 or more with us."

I had to consciously refocus my attention on his voice over the ringing in my ears.

He was referring to the fines, redress payments and administration costs of rectifying the decades of past mis-selling scandals.

A better solution was not to mis-sell, but banks are notorious for avoiding the better solution. Instead they had decided, future bank profits would be found through trading debt…

"This way," my colleague surmised, "we can take conduct risk off the books and post a short-term profit for shareholders. Then we focus instead on the lending—with interest rates as they are for the foreseeable, that's where the margins will be."

The UK banks laid off all financial advisers (which totalled in the range of over 10,000 professionals). This left 95% of the population disintermediated, orphaned and underserved. Trapped with rising debt levels and zero incentive to save.

A decade earlier I had given UK retail investors access and control over their wealth. They now had power over their piece of the economic system. However, even with this power placed at their fingertips, after years of mistrust in their banks, many still chose not to press the button.

Throughout my career, I had built a reputation for being the Robin Hood of the financial services industry. My quest was to inspire and empower retail investors. My final piece of the puzzle was to devolve power to the people so they would feel inclined to *press that button!*

My method was a proposal to deliver something that mattered most to retail investors—as it turned out this mattered least to the banks. That something, as we have already encountered, was *trust*.

The regulator's imminent ban on commission in the UK retail investment market meant that financial advisers could no longer earn revenues from selling products.

Something had to give. Something had to change.

I did not expect the board to reject my proposal—to create trusted advisers who would *plan the client* before planning the money, please customers by not mis-selling them and generate higher revenues for the bank at lower risk. It was the ultimate win-win scenario. But I was blind to the bigger picture.

Blind to the notion of boards across UK banking corporations, following one another like lemmings over a cliff, when Disney filmmakers are nearby… to lay off over 10,000 bank advisers across the entire industry. And disintermediate 95% of the population in the process.

The underservice was terrifying.

Three in five people had less than £5,000 in savings—just two months away from hardship.

Banking culture includes publishing quarterly reports for the City. The key focus of all *customer proposition teams* is to provide good numbers for that report. Resources would be injected into the product lines to deliver the best set of numbers. With interest rates frozen at historic low levels, this has been lending, for over a decade.

Condemning people, through fear, to a lifetime's prison sentence of unsecured debt—debt to the tune of half a household's total income. Matters were only going to get worse for the public. And, worse still for their kids: saddled with tuition fee debt and excluded from the property ladder.

As the words sank in, I realised I had not experienced this level of disparity between my own values and those of the banking industry since my time with RBS (Royal Bank of Scotland) several years earlier.

RBS hired me in 2005 to launch a SIPP—a self-invested personal pension scheme.

They saw it as a vehicle to hoover assets from other providers. I conducted a thorough feasibility study and showed them risk and forecast potential losses. We pulled the plug on the project, which was the first nail in my coffin.

Having angered the bosses, they made me redundant just six months after relocating me from Coventry to Edinburgh!

I was offered a second chance when rehired as head of investments.

The retail investment division of RBS was a joint venture with Aviva, who asked me to recommend a platform. A *platform* is a back office computer system that does not need to talk to other systems—Aviva ran over 200 platforms! I suggested one run by Scottish Friendly and the RBS bosses were so embarrassed they gave me a verbal warning.

The idea of deciding upon a small company to such a giant of a company was beyond their comprehension. Although, Aviva were later to take me up on my suggestion and it saved their bacon!

After this RBS asked me to investigate retail multi-asset funds, where I came across an in-house capability of Coutts bank (the Queen's bank). An equivalent fund would offer the public power over their finances.

Again, my recommendation was ignored, with Aviva purchasing Close Brothers. Their strategy was to stuff clients into a single fund manager with high-cost active funds.

The ethos of the banking world is never to wake people from the bondage they are born into. The prison they cannot smell, taste or touch. The prison of the mind. Anybody who dares suggest any other way forward is quickly and quietly discarded.

RBS made me redundant with a farewell message of not being *alpha male enough* for their organisation. I was too *nice* to my colleagues, because I refused to bully them. Yet, they had my five-year strategy for the business and did not need someone on my salary to implement it.

This was how I ended up as head of investments at HSBC, where I launched a retail multi-asset fund using HSBC's in-house capability. This took HSBC to being a market-leading fund provider and market-leading ISA (Individual Savings Account) provider—on the way, picking up the Personal Finance Award for best ISA.

I was responsible for £1 billion in sales for year one and again in year two, and rolled World Selection out to twenty-six markets globally.

This success was repeated with the discretionary management service, PIMS, the following year. Trouncing the competition whilst delivering great outcomes for customers.

The launch of the HSBC Global Investment Centre (the first bank platform) meant that, when all the other banks later laid off every single adviser, HSBC could carry on providing investments to retail customers. RBS on the other hand were caught in a compromising situation!

My RBS boss, who had systematically and repeatedly bullied me, was now sending me his CV asking for a job! There was a momentary glimmer where I wanted to grill him over an interview. In reality, I chose the waste basket, demonstrating the very kindness for which he had terminated my employment.

During the Money Marketing Awards in 2009, the HSBC table was next to that of RBS. This prestigious black-tie event coincided with the banking crisis, where RBS was bailed out by taxpayers, whereas HSBC was not. The difference between banks surviving, and those that did not, was ethics.

When the key guest speaker, comedian Dara O'Briain, took to the stage, he ripped constantly into RBS throughout his performance. It was hilarious, although my former colleagues on the next table failed to see the funny side!

In 2018, I had the pleasure of presenting my research findings in person to MPs and Lords at the House of Commons, as they sought to set up an All-Party Parliamentary Group on Financial Stability. Ten years on from the banking crisis—what lessons had been learnt?

My report highlighted continued failings in codes of conduct across the financial services industry.

Whilst your bank continues to extract value from you at the expense of the life you want, you will continue to mistrust them. You can, however, trust yourself to plan your financial wealth, health and success.

When you have developed a financial strategy, not only to survive, but to self-actualise, the banks must listen. They will take note and change their ways or they will die.

It is my mission—my life purpose—to help you achieve this.

When you have invested time in designing a plan through the method I will reveal to you, you will no longer suffer the irritations of anyone extracting value from your actions. No more pushy salespeople, overcharging, dishonesty or unsuitable products. No more funding human rights abuse, environmental exploitation or animal cruelty.

When you live from moment to moment, according to the values of others, you are faced with a choice between your money or your life.

It seems as if you can only have either one or the other. Possibly you pursue *value* and compromise your *values*. Potentially you pursue your *values* and discover that *value* eludes you. I call this the *Lower Way*.

It is your right to demand your money *and* your life!

To demand greater financial security, whilst making the most of your life. I call this the *Higher Way*.

Here we explore the lessons necessary to take you from living the lower way (basic needs—limited living—conditioned and controlled by bankers) to the higher way (self-actualised success—unlimited living—financially free from the chokehold of the banks).

It is important to remember that these paths are not exclusive—to live your best life you need to live the higher way, whilst still being able to navigate the lower way. For this is not about stuffing money into a mattress! We need banks… and we need banks to change to a higher way.

As you become accustomed to differentiating the Lower and Higher Ways, you will discover how to avoid the *Higher-Way Robbers*: the people, organisations and schemes that seek to rob you of your value and your values.

For every person, this path is different. It depends on who you are and how you view the world as well as what your unique skills and experiences are. The strategy you create, based on the values you possess, will be unique to you.

The bankers run *customer segmentation models* that predict how they can extract profits from you over a lifetime. There are multiple classifications of customer segments. Simply put, there are two core segments: *Haves* and *Have Nots*.

The model is optimised for profit by setting your goals for you.

The model predicts that the *Haves* accumulate wealth over a working life, crystallise and begin to decumulate wealth throughout retirement, leaving a succession nest egg on death. Throughout, the bankers offer products to protect wealth.

The model predicts the *Have Nots* will remain debt slaves throughout their lifetime, adjusting their marketing strategy accordingly. Your customer segment will appear on screen as the teller talks to you, so that they know the script.

Understand this: both segments are very profitable to the banks. And it is in their interest for you to conform to the role they have assigned you.

The truth is you neither want to be trapped in the rat race on the treadmill of work existence, blindly chasing money to the grave on the bet you can buy freedom later. Nor do you want a lifetime of debt slavery, surviving a meagre existence from one pay cheque to the next. Only two cheques away from crippling disaster.

The bankers, regulators and policymakers set the scripts. They actively compel the tellers and advisers to deliver the script without deviation to make sure you conform to their model. Bankers refer to this as *suitability*.

This is coded into their face-to-face processes, and even their automated systems. Bankers have even colluded with regulators to set this model in an international standard that all advisers must learn and follow. This is called ISO 22222.

Advisers dare not deviate from the standard, as to do so would face the wrath of bosses and regulators.

However, these are lower-way models!

These one-size-fits-all models do not explore how people truly want to fill their lives. Bankers refer to the process as *needs analysis*. In reality, our genuine needs are not analysed. They merely mitigate conduct risk for the bank, pay bankers bonuses and generate profit for bank shareholders.

Half of the population are not sure they are in the right career. Four in ten plan to change career in the next two years. One in three do not enjoy their work. Almost half admit their career is not fulfilling. One in three want a better work-life balance.

Many people never escape the treadmill of their work existence. Time ekes away, whilst one in four say they could not afford to switch jobs. One in five thought they were too old to start over.

Fear of financial security creates wage slavery. People deny their abilities and talents, and they ignore the purpose for which they were born. They create a void within themselves and in the emptiness of that void they feel pain.

Over time the pain gets worse, leading to the adoption of strategies to numb the pain or distract from addressing the root cause. They increase their level of debt. They grow weary as they remain weak, ineffective and grow older.

As they encounter one obstacle after the next, they start to lose direction and momentum. Eventually becoming powerless to stop the inevitable. They are stuck in the ways of the world, unsuited to their unique gifts and experiences. They live conditioned, in the shadows of lack and limitation.

They live in their psychological prison—the quality of their relationships with others and with the world diminishes. They experience troubling emotions. Their life seems repetitive, familiar and boring. They remain uninspired by life and destined for a bad death…

A deathbed full of regrets.

The only beneficiaries of this scenario are the banks.

The bankers want people on the treadmill and are so effective at keeping us on the never-ending slog, they have profoundly influenced society to ensure this happens from birth to grave.

From generation to generation, parents hand down the mantle of the lower way. Our employers, government and preferred media outlets push the same agenda. Even our schools reward memory and compliance over critical thinking. Critical thinking derails the machine.

Unlike the financial institutions and their one-solution-fits-all approach, you must first identify your unique needs and talents before even attempting to create your specific strategy.

This is rather like a game—a board game where each person has a slightly different strategy to the others. Through navigating the board, with all its obstacles, rewards, failures and successes, gamers develop a GAME plan.

This plan is the blueprint for your own plan—a strategy that is not simply a financial plan, but a life plan. A life plan for a better life and a better death.

The best investment you can make is in finding your personal freedom. Through the GAME Plan, I offer you my expertise from the banking arena and demonstrate how you can master your thoughts, actions, feelings and beliefs to harness that personal freedom for yourself.

As you master your finances, I will show you how to be all you want to be in the world. I will reveal how you put in place the financial means needed to support you and your family, whilst you pursue the life you love.

I will reveal the secrets that I was forbidden to show when I was a part of that banking world—and by doing so, we can expose that what the banks want people to believe is nothing more than a clever and complex scam designed to deceive us all.

And whilst I can act as your guide on the higher way, the best place to find a helping hand is at the end of your own arm!

PART TWO

MORE THAN A ROLL OF THE DICE

Imagine abundance.

Imagine you have the ability to improve the measure of anything in your life tenfold. Anything you want. And this ability can never be exhausted. You can use it on your bank accounts, your happiness, your love life, your intelligence, anything. It is entirely up to you.

You can create a clear sense of wealth in your thoughts, your needs, your feelings and your very being. You can develop wealth through your work, through your behaviours, through the way you live your life. And you even have the power to manifest wealth in your bank account.

Now, there are many personal and professional development gurus in the world who make similar claims. And for some people this works perfectly well. Through reading books and adopting different strategies around the habits of effective people, eating frogs and vision boards, they improve their lives.

However, whilst several of these methods are sound within themselves, they are all based on a fundamental lie—the lie which the banks have seeded and manipulated their customers with for decades. The lie does not stop the plethora of other methods from working—it has simply trained you into blindness.

The blindness of not seeing when you are being manipulated. The blindness of chasing temporary fixes—made temporary by your expectations and fears, rather than the actual longevity of the fix. And the blindness of wanting things that benefit your bank more than you.

You are always battling against those who do not want you to hold your nerve. Those who employ covert and deeply ingrained social strategies to sabotage your best efforts. Those whose voices whisper in your ear every single day.

Murmuring a message to buy into that terrifying apprehension around risk… Then buying into something to mask the fear— an expensive impulse purchase or a financial service that enables you to momentarily feel a little more secure about your money.

And whilst the widely available information on living a better life is not exactly hard to happen upon, the fact that the financial industry, politics, the media and by default, just about everything else is set up for you to fail, requires you to have something more.

Unless you're one of the people who can thrive in an essentially corrupt system (and the fact you are reading this book suggests you are not), you first need to recognise the lie and understand how it affects you (and others). Then you need to create ways of negating it from all future plans.

The key concepts here are not flights of fancy. These are real-world solutions—based on facts and figures and well-documented results that have touched the lives of millions throughout the world.

Grounded in a physical strategy and based on provable experience, the financial architecture you put into place here is tried and tested (then frequently squirrelled away for being too beneficial) by the UK's biggest banking giants. It is grounded in money! And it is greater than all these.

These are not only centred around money, they encompass every aspect of your life. So, we are focused on values-driven financial planning—and more importantly directed towards *life planning*.

Life planning can truly empower you to run your money and your life—it will unlock the means to live the life of your dreams freely.

When navigating the treacherous landscape of the financial services industry, I recommend avoiding the bank-designed traps of jargon and purposefully complex routes in favour of making it fun! So, I use a life planning process through playing the board game, *Your Money or Your Life!*

This dramatic and fun adventure involves gathering treasures, while avoiding highway robbers and higher-way robbers alike. As you navigate the game, you will reveal the issues impacting your life and explore the solutions to your challenges.

Maybe you find yourself in a pit of debt and despair. Perhaps the banking crisis has destroyed best-laid financial plans, while the financial turbulence and austerity that followed may have hindered your recovery. Possibly you are saddled with debt and the prospects for future generations are looking bleak.

Potentially, you may find your lifestyle and finances have locked you into a treadmill of work existence. Possibly a fear of financial insecurity blocks your path to freedom. A feeling of being unfulfilled and desperate emptiness may warn you of a life wasted, slowly ebbing away. You may be struggling with the hopelessness of it all.

The human lifetime is merely the blink of an eye.

A brief glimmer in the darkness.

Apart from Japan, average life expectancy is less than one thousand months. And whilst this may seem a lot, many of those months are behind you. Gone forever—resigned to memories.

When you calculate how many months you have lived and subtract this amount from the estimated life expectancy of your country, the figure you are left with is painfully low. So low in fact that many are crippled by how little time they have remaining on this Earth.

They want to do something different with their lives and feel they cannot. Time is running out. Problems appear insurmountable. So, they do not even begin. They accept where they are. Accept their lot.

They settle for what they have. Make the best of it all. They decide this is just the way it is. And, before the world knocks it out of them, they push down any feelings which suggest they could do better. It is what it is.

They are told to forget their dreams, needs and ambitions. They tell themselves to forget their dreams, needs and ambitions.

They read it in the papers, see it on the news, experience it throughout the media. Parents tell their children to *get a proper job like everyone else* and to earn a living. Teachers say it, bosses say it, everybody says it. That is just what *it's like in the real world* and if you *want to get ahead*, there is a particular way of acting.

The limited version of the world is so deeply ingrained; people believe it without question. And if they do not, society labels them *odd*, believing there is something very wrong with them.

An even greater challenge here is you are hardwired to accept information that supports your own worldview. You will literally filter out anything that contrasts or conflicts from that integral perspective. Even to the extremes of believing *fake news* and *alternative facts*!

When we encounter the very thing that can change our lives for the better, we usually fail to even acknowledge its existence. Therefore, it is not until some catastrophe or all-encompassing change shatters our existing worldview that we become sensitised to those transformative nuggets of wisdom that offer real change.

People across the globe live as others expect them to live. They do what they must do to survive. They fail to do what they are good at or enjoy in favour of an indoctrination by society—to live as a normal person. Humanity pats them on the back for being a *good citizen*. Until, eventually, they lose inspiration and live a bland, ordinary life.

When they do this, the genius they were born to be is never born. And they go to their death, ordinary and unnoticed.

A glimmer in the darkness that everybody missed.

Look at the life you have before you. Life expectancy in the UK is 81.6 years.

or Your Life

Country	Life expectancy months	Retirement Age	Retirement months
India	760	65	20
China	871	60 men 50 women	151 men 271 women
US	944	67 by 2027	140
Australia	959	67 by 2023	155
UK	979	68 by 2037	163
Japan	1,006	60	286

Be optimistic and say you live for a thousand months. The big questions are:

- How many months have you lived and how many months do you have left?

- How well do you plan to live them?

- How many months at work?

- How many in a job you hate?

- How many in a job you love?

- How many months do you have in retirement (when state pension benefits begin)?

The concept of *retirement* no longer exists. The notion that you have a substantial period of rest beyond your working life is outdated. Most pensioners partake in work in one form or another—out of choice or sometimes otherwise—whether that be paid or unpaid.

Retirement is today a blessing for a privileged few who disliked their jobs, but were duped into staying at them until they could afford to rest. Yet, rather than buy into the retirement myth we are sold, many a happy millionaire works into their eighties.

A better viewpoint is that of *financial freedom*—the period when you can buy yourself the leisure time to do as you please with your life. Many take the risk of buying financial freedom in later life.

Those who spend their prime years of health and vitality in the service of this ethos fail to realise how close financial freedom is for us all. They are sold the idea that it isn't, by the banks. And the lie keeps them squandering their lifetime in a job they hate.

Those inseparable bedfellows of bankers and politicians, have even made it compulsory in the UK that you buy freedom in later life through workplace pensions. Life savings are locked away until old age. Then taxed. Whilst simultaneously, government offers means-tested state pension benefits, so you are penalised for your aspirations.

Yes, we are lower-way tax slaves from childhood till death (and beyond). However, there remains a chance that you can end wage slavery earlier than you have been led to believe. Your financial freedom is close at hand.

There are ways you can generate income from what you love to do (and from which you never want to retire) to replace wage slavery, in very little time.

You have been trained into handing over your life savings to bankers who are paid big bonuses from the hidden fees. You pass control of your money to bankers who make decisions for you.

Every unit of money you spend or invest is a powerful vote for the change you want to see in the world. Bankers and CEOs vote by proxy— for arms, genocide, oil, deforestation, pollution, human exploitation, species extinction, destruction of the planet and other aspects of slow, gradual annihilation.

Thus, you are indoctrinated into servicing big corporations with their false promises about performance. Whilst they perpetrate human exploitation or destruction of the planet, you are taught to support warmongering government coffers.

The solution can be found with *values-based investments*.

Values-based investing is putting your money where your mouth is. It is the umbrella term for socially responsible investing, environmental social governance investing and impact investing.

It is one of the newest and fastest-growing sectors within the investment world.

Two in three of us believe it delivers the same or better returns than standard investments. Half of us boycott companies or brands because we disagree with ethics of corporate behaviour[2].

Younger generations embrace values. When asked if social or environmental impact is important to their investment decisions, 85% of millennials agreed, compared to 70% of Generation X, and 49% of baby boomers[3].

The outlook for the future looks bright. The outlook looks values based.

Corporate bosses are now required to report on environmental, social and governance factors in annual returns. They no longer need to fear the wrath of shareholders for tabling proposals to eliminate the use of fossil fuels that may negatively impact their bottom line.

Dr Raj Sisodia, co-founder of *Conscious Capitalism*, pioneered research that shows values-based organisations outperform the market (as measured by the S&P 500 index). These *Firms of Endearment*[4] outperform the market both in the short term and long term. And, they outperform by a staggering 14:1.

In the business world, values equate to a staggering generation of turnover!

There are four tenets these values-based businesses share. Four tenets which are directly linked to the outperformance over other organisations. These are:

- **Purpose:** they each have a greater purpose

- **People:** the culture of people within the organisation

- **Planet:** the overarching benefits to the global ecosystem

- **Profit:** servant leadership for the benefit of stakeholders

Profit is mental.

Not that we are mad to seek profit, rather it is an intellectual concept.

Intellectual capital is an asset—broadly defined as *the collection of all informational resources a company possesses.* These are employed to drive profits.

Leadership is the exercise of intellectual power in an organisation for the management of the assets, resources, finances, income, expenditure and profit.

Leadership drives profit for the benefit of stakeholders.

Servant leadership shares power and puts the needs of all stakeholders on an equal footing. It helps people perform as highly as possible for the benefit of all stakeholders. Dr Sisodia's study shows that servant leadership is a key tenet that drives higher sustainable profits.

Profit is money. Money is not a physical object, although it may be exchanged for physical objects. It is an intellectual measure of economic value. Money is a 3,500-year-old human invention. A total fabrication of the human mind.

Money, like profit, is mental.

And only humans use money to pay for living on Earth!

Money was invented to facilitate the sharing and exchange of goods and services among individuals and groups of people. Therefore, money management is a mental construct, not a physical one.

Money was once physically represented in the form of shells, stones, ingots of precious metal or paper bills. Today, it is a blip on a banker's computer screen.

When you are granted a loan, the banker does not go down to the vault to set aside a gold bar, they simply enter the amount on their computer. You or I would be arrested for printing money, but this is how the banks do it!

Money is a mere promise. It represents a promise by the issuer to deliver to the bearer on demand physical objects of equivalent value. A promise that we trust, sometimes with good reason and sometimes foolishly. We trust the promise will be honoured in the future.

Again, trust!

When we move an organisation from imbalance to balance on the foundations of purpose, people, planet and profit, we observe a more than tenfold financial outperformance. We additionally create wealth that is cultural and spiritual, social and emotional, physical and ecological, intellectual and financial.

If you are looking to invest in values-based organisations, nearly all mutual funds have signed up to the UN Principles for Responsible Investment initiative (PRI). Signatories must report on environmental, social and governance (ESG) criteria. This data is available to you, which makes it easier for you to choose values-based investments.

Think about it.

People and planet must now be considered and reported on by fund managers.

Virtually the entire world of investments must disclose what they are doing to heal world grief. How amazing is that?

ESG criteria is a set of standards for a company's operations that socially-conscious investors use to screen investments.

Environmental criteria look at how a company performs as a steward of the natural environment. Social criteria examine how a company manages relationships with its employees, suppliers, customers and the communities where it operates. Governance deals with a company's leadership, executive pay, audits, internal controls and shareholder rights.

Fund managers are moving towards the incorporation of ESG factors in investment decision-making through screening, integration, thematic investments and active ownership.

Here is a secret that the City does not want you to know… Market analysts agree, values-based organisations deliver as good as, or often better returns than the market in general. High ESG-rated companies show higher profitability; higher dividend yield and lower business-specific tail risks than the market.

Blockchain technology is also evolving ESG reporting so the information can be trusted. Currently, the data is owned by those who generate it, although with blockchain the data sits in the public domain and cannot be tampered with. It becomes a permanent public record at creation.

The four key business areas—purpose, people, planet and profit—can be applied to your own personal and professional core values. When you adapt the four tenets to your own approach to life, you become values based. People who are led by a set of powerful, benevolent values, generate sustainable wealth in many aspects of their lives.

The four tenets of people who outperform, by no coincidence, stem from the same four factors:

Planet—Physical (The body of your life)

People—Emotional (The heart of your life)

Profit—Cerebral (The mind of your life)

Purpose—Mission (The spirit of your life)

It works at a corporate level, an investment level and a personal level.

Depending on your unique make up, you have a leading domain of human performance—an alchemy of four distinct intelligences that offers you superpowers in certain areas. These four intelligences are:

- Rational (IQ)

- Spiritual (SQ)

- Emotional (EQ)

- Physical (PQ)

The four intelligences act upon contrasting aspects of being human. Our IQ is a measure of the *mental body*—our logical minds and intellect. The PQ quantifies the *physical body*—instinct. EQ symbolises the *emotional body*—heart and feelings. And SQ indicates a measurement of *spiritual body*—values and intuition.

On the gaming board of *Your Money or Your Life!* these four measures act as the main compass points or regions by which we navigate. Depending on your unique combination of intelligence, you will naturally gravitate to and resonate with some areas of the board over others.

PLANET (PHYSICAL OR BODY)

Body relates to our physical matter, gut instinct and the subconscious.

The body of our life is our breath—our fundamental need. It is being human in the world through our heritage—the lineage that extends from you, to all your ancestors. The cycle of lifetimes (since prehistoric times) which forms everything you are born into this world with.

Each lifetime is a part of a wider natural cycle, a continuous organic process of birth, death and rebirth through future generations.

The body and planet are one and the same; they include matter in various forms: solids, liquids, gases, ether, energy and the forces that hold our universe together (or pull it apart!).

And this extends to the *things* around us; the things we crave, the things we need and the things that divert our attention from other aspects of our lives.

Gut instinct is derived from our lizard brain—the amygdala—a mechanism that compels us to survive. To meet our physical, essential needs, such as food, water and shelter. It protects us from danger, repels us from harm and causes us to constantly be seeking *more*.

Physical intelligence (PQ) is the ability to master our gut instinct and to use the body in highly differentiated, skilled ways. These can be for both goal-oriented and expressive purposes, such as the athlete, in tune with their body, so they can instantly respond with agility, strength, speed or endurance.

As with all four tenets, an over-emphasis on body can create a life imbalance. Blindly following gut instinct can be dangerous. Our goal is not simply to survive—it is to live a deeply meaningful life.

PEOPLE (EMOTIONAL OR HEART)

Heart encompasses our feelings, our emotions. The sometimes gentle whisperer, other times thunderous roar. The metaphor of the heart is of a self-transcending organ. A physical, beating drum that measures our lifetime, yet symbolises compassion, loving kindness and generosity.

Seated in the medulla oblongata, emotions are the chemical compass that help us navigate through life and our physical world. Hormones and neurochemical cocktails that compel us towards or away from specific situations or circumstances.

We all know the icy fingers of terror and the uncontainable fire of anger. And many of us know the knotted, twisted warmth of love; the delightful comfort of being in love and the pleasure it creates. An untethered joy which spills out, beyond our own lifetime.

Whilst forging a clear way forward, in many cases the emotional heart can also become overwhelmed and confused when we rely too greatly upon it (at the expense of the other tenets). In contrast, suppressing emotions can lead to a disconnection from feelings: numbing, depressing and forming an essentially empty life, devoid of heart.

A life without care for others motivates a person into action for themselves—the narcissist, the psychopath and the banker.

Emotional intelligence (EQ) is our ability to identify and manage our emotions and the emotions of others. The art of carer and nurturer, who can navigate difficult situations through empathy, compassion and a heartfelt sense of direction.

An over-emphasis on emotions or heart will develop a life-imbalanced and turmoil.

Following the heart alone can lead to severe depression, a sense of overwhelm and lack of greater context in life. Our goal is not simply to connect with others, our goal is to relate to others in collaboration—a shared vision for our shared planet.

PROFIT (CEREBRAL OR MIND)

Mind refers to our intellectual nature. The champion of self-enhancement and complex thinking, the mind is both rational and intellectual capable of endless wonders and infinite horrors. It can help us achieve more in life than the moments of our lifetime and it can dominate us into submission and slavery.

The mind deals in constructs and frameworks, philosophy and ethos, creation and imagination. It is the higher-level thought that exists beyond the mentality of *I want* and *fight or flight*.

Associated with the connective tissue within our brains, the mind is capable of truly wondrous things. Yet, as with all imbalance, the overused, overwhelmed mind becomes challenging.

Without the informed guidance from the heart, the mind can be cold, calculating and without concern for others. With no spirit, the mind loses sight of the greater mission, the higher purpose and wider vision we were born into this world to achieve.

Failing to balance mind and body can cause us to neglect our basic needs, whilst forgetting that we are part of an ecosystem… when that system fails, we die.

An over-emphasis of mind in self-enhancement and protecting one's own interests leads to a shallow existence and an empty death. Creation without purpose, philosophy without grounding and acquisition without feeling cause a misappropriation of the life we have, just *more* in a world that does not need *more*.

However, the mind is a crucible of potential—a bubbling cauldron of all that is unique in humankind. When we apply Intellectual Intelligence (IQ) in a balanced and harmonious way, we birth something far greater than ourselves: not simply *more*, but rather, innovative, imaginative and inspirational.

PURPOSE (MISSION OR SPIRIT)

Traditionally, spirit is viewed to be supernatural in origin, older than the heart and wiser than the mind. Spirit is an interconnected life force, the spark of creation. It is believed to connect us with others and with a higher power in ways that go beyond our physical nature.

Spirit evokes a sense of greater meaning, long-term purpose and deeper values. And spirit can also be the core of something: its essence and its potential to achieve something beyond the confines and context of its own limitation.

It is your ability to become more than your lifetime suggests. It is how an investment can reap more rewards than the time or resources invested in it. Spirit is how every moment can last eternally and how everyone champions a legacy. A legacy, which by design or default, will manifest itself in the world.

Leaders of indigenous faiths expressed a connection to *Great Nature*. For thousands of years, through deep inner inquiry, philosophers and sages have mapped their world context onto the unknown. Through this pursuit we have come to the realisation that we, God, the universe, all things, are one and the same.

Spiritual intelligence (SQ) is transpersonal—it exists beyond the self and the material, corporeal world. It is ethereal and yet, utterly innate to all things. It guides us through the broader questions in life, the quandaries and paradoxes.

Spirit could be viewed as something *greater than*. Greater than the sum of its parts, greater in influence than its physical nature, greater in depth of feeling than its emotion, greater in ideals than its own mind. Spirit is greater in each moment than the time possessed by that moment and greater in longevity than the lifetime through which it was experienced.

Our PQ sees an acorn as food, our EQ feels the acorn as the tree it can become, our IQ imagines an acorn as a forest, yet our SQ knows that little acorn contains all things that exist in the universe.

An over-emphasis on spirit throws us into imbalance, for our goal is not to live on a bed of nails, eating grains of rice in the hope of connecting with some divine source. Our mission is to be present through a physical body, in the pursuit of a unique purpose—the purpose we were born to create. And in doing so, to retain our connection to all people and all we truly are.

Our life purpose is to experience being human: engaged in mind, body, heart and spirit. To bring all these aspects of ourselves into the physical, material world. To share our story of success, happiness and meaning as a stepping stone for all those who are yet to come.

As values-led businesses are motivated to by the four P's of Planet, People, Profit and Purpose, we are driven by a fire to be who we were born to be: body, heart, mind and spirit. As a parallel to the four sides of a die, these tenets support each other, giving structure to each face from one to six and overall.

And when a person is missing one of these four tenets, it results in a pain that resonates throughout every aspect of their being. A pain so powerful, they hunger for *more* to mask it, quench it, rip it from their lives—and by doing so, they rip out the very person they were born to be.

With a solid structure, dice cannot exist. They cannot be rolled. The game cannot be played.

In which of these *intelligences* do you reside consciously most of the time?

If we reside primarily in one aspect, at the expense of other aspects, we tumble into a state of imbalance. When gripped by this imbalance we experience fear, anxiety, chaos, hunger and despondency.

However, these emotions are not bad. Their presence and acknowledgement is merely an indicator that we need to restore balance. In Shinto philosophy, there are no bad emotions: simply motivators to ensure we remain on the best path.

When confronted with the provocation of powerful emotions, most people do not know how to move from imbalance to balance, so they fixate on the feeling, rather than a solution.

For example, those who reside primarily in logical mind have little connection to the feeling centres of emotional and spiritual consciousness. They are aware of emotions and conscience but are not moved by them. They may be rich at the bank, but not in the heart.

Whereas, those who reside primarily in a profoundly creative perspective have little grounding in a practical or intellectual sense. They may live with an open heart and empty pockets.

There are individuals who seek to enhance only themselves. Without a strong connection to others or the slightest care for anybody else, they are locked into a world which revolves only around them. Manipulating and controlling.

Then there are people who live a life of self-transcendence. By giving to others at the expense of their own essential needs, they allow themselves to be controlled: having their reality dictated for them. They become locked up in a tiny room, limited and never giving themselves space to grow or flourish. Manipulated and dominated.

People who are in a state of imbalance feel pain from a deep wound of disparity. It hurts them intensely and causes them agony and anguish. When allowed to continue unchecked, they endure prolonged periods of emotional suffering.

Eventually, if they fail to correct their course, they enter a depressive state and experience an overall feeling of helplessness, a dark pit of despair. Trapped and completely alone they are unable to escape the ever-rotating spiral of shame and isolation.

The internal pain worsens, the psychological battle escalates, they rationalise that they need to take drastic action to escape the ties that bind them. To overcome their fears, they engage, make rash, angry decisions as they fight their environment and slap away every helping hand.

Alternatively, they may instinctively take flight from the very things that would provide some form of resolution, making drastic ill-considered life changes. They become stuck in a rut or freeze completely, trapped in a paralysed state of indecision. They may even resort to self-harm, addiction or contemplate ending it all.

In the UK there are 500 suicides every month, that's almost one every hour.

When we explore why this epidemic exists through a lens of balance, we discover how mind, body, heart and spirit play an important part in appreciating the problems and understanding the solutions.

The imbalanced mind takes the form of mental health problems such as anxiety, various forms of depression, OCD or psychosis.

A physical imbalance is revealed through long-term pain or illness, difficulties when adjusting to a tremendous change such as retirement or redundancy, money problems, homelessness, addiction, substance abuse and developing relationships based upon sexual or physical abuse.

The imbalanced heart beats to the rhythm of bullying, discrimination, domestic abuse, bereavement, broken relationships, isolation, loneliness, losing a loved one to suicide or unwanted/forced marriage.

For the spirit, an imbalanced life is an inescapable prison: trapped by feeling inadequate, a failure, doubts or denial about sexual and gender identity, hatred of others based on religious dogma or prejudice—adrift, without a sense of greater purpose, life mission or birthright.

Deficiency in any element means imbalance for the whole. Lack in any of the four tenets saturates the entire person. The imbalance permeates our every action, behaviour and decision until we cannot even differentiate what restores balance from what exacerbates the problem.

The answer can be found by engaging your four intelligences and removing poverty in every aspect of your life; every *body of your being*.

Equilibrium is finding comfort in *enough*. Enough for your mind, body, heart and spirit—as when you have *enough* for the whole, you navigate a balanced path: a higher way.

What areas of your life do you need to focus on to find your higher way?

What areas are you currently focusing too much upon—what is distracting you from your higher way?

At the very core of this ethos are your values. Values are the central stem on a set of scales—the gravitational centre for balance and alignment. Alignment of your unique talents with the actions you take, pivot the scales into balance around a core of values.

We are told to place a self-imposed limit on how much abundance we might possess. Shown time and time again how abundance is something only a select few can attain, because it is limited and scarce. However, self-imposed limits are mind-imposed limits, because limits, like money, are mental.

We live, bombarded by the propaganda of abundance as a quantifiable and finite thing. Yet abundance is a state of mind—the paradigm of balance, through which we fulfil our essential needs and by which we self-actualise in the creation of an effective legacy. A legacy that stems from a finite lifetime into a quantifiable value that is greater than a lifetime.

Most people never achieve a conscious legacy, abundance or even balance. Not because they couldn't, but simply because they were told they couldn't. And to go against the expected norm is uncomfortable.

Domesticated by discomfort, people seek quick fixes to numb the pain and make them feel comfortable again. They do not use their unique gifts and talents, but instead, they stay in a small box. Limited by mindset, they plonk themselves down on a metaphorical (or literal) sofa and watch time pass by, like a countdown to the end of life.

When you walk a higher way, you live a life that is bigger than your life.

It is easy for us to stare at the path in front of our feet; to care only for oneself or to look after others at the expense of oneself. Turning attention to the impact you can have on the lives of others results in moments of life that have a greater effect on the world than the time you put into those moments.

Ponder the changes you can make for the planet, changes that last long after you are gone. People are easily forgotten. Living unconsciously, most find themselves lost, their contribution to the world is fleeting, weak and ineffective. As a result, success eludes them in life.

They are condemned to struggle with a mundane, ordinary existence from one day to the next. Their potential is spent on time-wasting pursuits where little is achieved. And when they die, they disappear from the world—leaving the world no better or worse for them ever being here.

To live a life dedicated to making benevolent, lasting change can be uncomfortable from time to time—you may need to go beyond what you feel capable of, you may need to prove yourself, you may need to change your perspective. Yet, a life spent without making any sort of real mark on the world you leave behind? To face your death without ever needing to be here?

If that is not more painful than a temporary discomfort to you, then you are not truly appreciating how hard death can be for those who die in the knowledge they never made a difference.

Be remembered.

Fulfil your potential consciously and as early as possible in your life. Make a pact with yourself to act from the genius within you. To make your life worthwhile from this point onwards.

Work is more than just *earning a living*—work is how you invest the years of your life, into a purpose that reaps greater rewards than the months of your life. Think about your life purpose and the work that you were born to do.

Very few take the time to think about the life they were born to live. Most people choose work based on the expectations of others: their parents, their teachers and society. Some people view the sole purpose of paid employment as getting paid.

They end up on a mundane treadmill of work existence for the best part of their lives. They are unhappy in their work. They hate Mondays. Love Fridays. They yearn for retirement.

Job haters gamble on being able to buy themselves freedom. The lottery ticket reads *enjoy freedom later*. Many stake their freedom on old age, often after retirement. Some make it there… countless thousands lose that bet!

They work fruitlessly in shadows, unproductive in their work. The prospect of financial freedom on the far horizon is some motivation, but is it really motivation enough? What if they could be out on parole in half the time?

Job haters fail to ascend through their work. They make no difference to the planet—so will not get a thank you card from the Earth when they leave. They fail to alleviate world grief in any meaningful way, opting instead, to simply survive. They chase money blindly to the grave.

I do not want you to tolerate a job you hate for one single day longer than you must.

Some argue the more you get paid the more time you will eventually have to pursue your mission. You are placed on a savings plan where income on eventual capital becomes sufficient to meet your daily expenses. Then at the crossing-point you leave the job you hate.

This method prolongs your stint on the treadmill of work existence.

There is no sense in dying with capital in the bank, unless you intend to pass it on to nearest and dearest (less deductions for the taxman). You could have left the job you hate in half the time by drawing down capital in later life.

It all begins with you knowing your greater purpose in life—your assignment, your mission—and aligning your work with it to create a vocation.

Leave the job you hate, start the job you love. Start the job you love even before you leave the job you hate. When we love our work, work does not feel like work any more. We are more productive, we reap economic benefits and we never want to retire.

There is another secret the City does not want you to know… A secret that has been held up as a foolish or silly thing to disempower it. Those in power have spent years making this secret seem ridiculous by telling us life must be a struggle, where poverty is the default unless we rely on the banks.

The secret is simple and yet powerful. If you apply parallels of the organisational principles to your life, by focusing on the tenets of mind, body, heart and soul, your finances have the capacity to improve tenfold.

You flourish. You thrive. You lead a life imbued with passion, purpose and creativity; love and compassion; material success and well-being; authority and manifestation.

How do you do this?

To understand the answer to this question, you need to explore yourself and your life in deeper and more detailed ways than you have before. By understanding your income, expenses, what you own and what you owe against your values as represented by your four tenet goals, you diminish what no longer serves you. You expand what supports who you want to be in the world.

The result is a movement towards abundance in life and money. However, this is just the beginning, because to see real change in your life, you cannot only function in isolation—you can also truly change in relation to the world around you.

If we change, our communities change. If we thrive, our communities thrive. If our communities thrive, we create a world of freedom, compassion, harmony and prosperity. We begin to heal world grief and our planet thrives.

Why does values-based living bring about such transformation?

Values-based living relies on having a purpose. For people without a purpose, life is mundane. They feel adrift. They scrabble around in the shadows. They hate what they do and who they are. They feel uninspired.

Without a purpose, how productive would you be? What's your earning potential?

Imagine you have a real purpose in life.

It activates you. It motivates you. It moves you to get up in the morning. It sustains you when times are tough. It serves as a guiding star to navigate by when you stray off course. You are focused, inspired, engaged and energised. The light within you is well and truly lit. You do what you're good at, what you love.

How productive might you be? What is your earning potential now?

We walk two paths—the lower way or the higher way. The lower way only focuses on the necessities—the resources you need to make ends meet and when you have those, the pursuit of more of those.

The higher way is the road of greater purpose, vision and abundance in a balanced approach. It is the path of the self-actualised and self-fulfilled pioneers who change the world for the better.

The Money or Your Life values-based system shows you how to travel the higher way for a happier, richer, nicer, better life. And this is not just a roll of the dice in connection to finances and money—by playing the game you explore every aspect of your life in a measurable and real-world way.

You might be wondering how an alignment with values can improve your love life. Well, have you ever been in a relationship where you are incompatible?

If so, you know how that feels!

Now, imagine if you had an immediate connection with your partner in all four tenets of mind, body, heart and spirit. Think about that relationship from the moment you meet, where you have intellectual compatibility, sexual chemistry, mutual unconditional love and shared values.

When it comes to relationships, many people only engage one or two forms of intelligence, whilst others apply their four intelligences in ways that are unhelpful. When you are navigating your way through relationships with all four intelligences applied in a balanced way, it fundamentally changes the way you live for the better.

You can also see remarkable improvements in your state of health by using a strategic, values-based approach to living. Your beliefs govern the decisions you make, which generate your actions. Over time, these actions become your natural behaviours and ultimately produce your lifestyle.

Healthy beliefs correspond to healthy lifestyles.

Imagine if you and your family value-aligned eating habits, fitness activities, mechanisms for coping with stress, emotional management, media consumption and getting out in nature.

It is not a case of… when you are happy, you are in balance. It is more accurate to say… when you are in balance, you are happy. Balance brings peace, fulfilment, well-being and prosperity into your life. When you are happy you are successful.

Whilst many believe that we are successful when we become happy, the reality is, when you are happy you become successful. Balance leads to happiness, leads to success. Balance is the route to abundance.

You have the power to manifest abundance in your health, love life and bank account.

Values create value. As values, so value!

PART THREE

MONEY'S NO OBJECT

The markets need a trusted adviser now more than ever.

At just after 8am on Monday 2nd January 2012, I was jogging along the Thames pathway from Limehouse to the Isle of Dogs. That moment has left an indelible mark on my psyche, because it was in that moment I experienced a deep and lasting shift within me.

The winter morning sun shone brightly. An aroma of sea-mist hung on the Thames at the morning high tide. Wash from passing boats splashed joyfully against the green concrete flood defence walls. Seagulls hung magically still in the wind to skilfully catch bread thrown by the lady with the blue coat. A row of cormorants held open their wings to dry as they stood magnificent on the jetty, contrasting starkly with distant wharfs and concrete towers.

Money's no object.

Money is not an obstacle—not something to fear or fall in love with. It is simply the means to an end... with the end being a life you love.

Long distance running creates a deep state of mindfulness. The strides form a rhythm. The rhythm transports you to the *zone*: a place where you experience flow. In this flow state, you achieve results that otherwise evade you and you are subject to an inner voice, a wise and knowing voice.

As my drumbeat steps pounded along the riverbank, I worried about a difficult and disturbing predicament at the banks. In that same moment, I experienced a paradoxical joy, because somewhere within I knew the answer—a prospect, so clear, yet one I struggled to face.

"Why did they turn down the project?" I pondered. "The pilot studies with the advisers were a resounding success! At both City and Canary Wharf branches!"

Customers had indeed offered a resounding chorus of approval—they said it had been the best financial conversation they had known in twenty-five years. I had created that elusive, *trusted adviser relationship*, for a dozen bank advisers and their clients. Despite proof of concept, the bank still said no.

"Once again Steve, you are ahead of your time!" A voice welled up within me. "For them a trusted adviser is too farfetched!"

Bankers possess a high quotient of mind intelligence and are just beginning to appreciate the need for emotional intelligence. When it comes to the seemingly impossible expanse of spiritual intelligence, they are somewhat lacking.

Bankers do not have a clear moral compass guiding their commercial decisions. They are not values based. It's just the lobby walls that say they are. So, in the absence of leadership taking a values-based approach, the system is at some point, doomed to fail!

"I head investments!" Step.

"I chair the industry steering group." Step.

"I have a qualified track record of successes under my belt." Step.

"I never saw this coming!" I replied to that mysterious voice within. "Where do I go from here? I can't change the system. The system is failing. The system will soon disappear. We need a new system. We need a whole new game plan!"

Despite empirical evidence demonstrating that trusted adviser relationships can be created profitably (for the least-trusted industry globally), the bank bosses had decided to throw in the towel on financial advice.

The board could not see how advisers would switch from commission and earn fees from giving advice: from treating the client as the customer, rather than the money as the customer.

Rather than solving the problem, the banks decided to just pull out completely. Laying off retail advisers and disintermediating the retail investor. The result of this would be ordinary people no longer having access to financial advice.

"Everyone will think I'm mad," I told myself as I jogged past the high-class riverside apartments along the Thames. "Not for having a whole conversation with myself, although that may be justification enough! But, for giving up a top job in the City, sacrificing everything, to attempt to build the new paradigm for financial planning!"

I had, essentially turned my back on the old way and created independently, a whole new game plan. A fool's errand?

Possibly—I had done this with my savings that would last only eighteen months.

"Follow your heart, Steve." That inner voice replied. "Yes. The way of conscience is a difficult path, as is any journey that is worth taking. Trust. Let go. Know that you will be looked after."

This new paradigm was my mission, my fire, my birthright—a whole new game plan that would reveal just how archaic and self-serving the banks' current approach is. It would loosen the chokehold they had on their customers and release people from the chains of control banks use every day to keep people poor (in more ways than just financial).

"If not you, who? If not now, when?" Step, step, step.

Have you ever heard a voice within telling you to take a step and your logical mind tells you that you are a fool for listening?

People frequently make excuses for not living their life purpose. From lack of money to what others may think, the reasons for not being who they were born to be are as large in amount as the wealth they could be enjoying.

I quit the banks there and then.

For the next five years, I strived to build the trusted advice firm I had foreseen in that moment. I took on the real and harsh world of small business, whilst lobbying institutions, parliament, regulators and the media for greater market integrity.

In all that time, I never could fathom why private investors were not queuing up for a piece of the action. Nor why institutions failed to show up to the market integrity meetings. What stopped private investors from wanting empowerment for retail investors?

At 11am on Friday 23rd June 2017 I was sat in a coffee shop opposite St Paul's cathedral on Ludgate Hill. Strong coffee aromas wafted around the crowded café, as my friend Glyn introduced me to Bill.

Bill was a private detective specialising in helping victims of financial crime. He looked like Lieutenant Columbo: short, stocky, late middle-aged, with an ill-fitting suit. Bill loved to talk.

"Lawyers litigate, detectives investigate," Bill told me. "Victims are wasting their time with lawyers. It takes them years just to get up to speed. By then the scammers have moved on. The victims end up spending a fortune on legal fees they can least afford. The scammers get away with it. The victims are devastated. It is all too much, resulting in many taking their own lives."

The warmth from the scent of coffee did nothing to ease the chill I felt as Bill continued. "The police and the Serious Fraud Office (SFO) can't help. The police are not equipped to tackle financial crime, while the SFO have sufficient funds to maintain only a small case load."

"The Government deliberately caps SFO funding to around 1% of the total annual proceeds of financial crime—embarrassing the City is not considered in the public interest! London is a key global financial capital and parliament simply won't risk it."

No wonder the City did not want me to succeed—giving people power over their finances?

Politicians place the system before the people and claim it is in the public interest to do so. The system views people as a source of revenue. It wants people on the treadmill of debt. Debt is where the margins are and that is how the system is funded.

Laura was 84 and a former teacher.

The caller sounded genuine, she was able to give her some details to make it sound like she was ringing from her bank. She told Laura the account had been compromised, and they suspected staff at the branch, so she even told her what to say if challenged by branch staff when making the withdrawal.

Her savings were so large she had to do it in three transactions over nearly two weeks, but staff only challenged her on one of the three occasions. In total, she lost over £200,000. The police were involved and Laura's solicitor investigated how the bank had breached its duty of care.

Banks have the duty to protect their customers—to ensure solid anti-money laundering checks when onboarding accounts. One would assume banks would be concerned that people are claiming accounts have been cloned, despite their anti-money laundering and transaction tracking processes.

However, banking fraud departments do not actively pursue or ensure attempted fraudsters are criminally prosecuted. They should have a mandatory duty to pursue every case. They do not. Fraudsters feel it is an almost risk-free activity, as the chances of being caught are minimal.

Poor tracking of suspicious activity for payments outside the normal pattern or receipts causes major issues when unusually sized transactions are received into accounts. Banks should be aware when these are *paid on* within a brief time in a recently opened account (e.g. less than say a year old).

Banks are not penalised for serious failings and there are no incentives for the banks to have an effective process. Banks have the Government in their pockets.

The UK National Audit Office (NAO) estimates that only twenty-six pence in every £100 stolen through financial crime is ever recovered. The City has a global reputation to maintain and is given free rein to achieve this.

And the Government turns a blind eye to scams and scandals, again using that ol' *public interest* chestnut as a defence. All the while, the legal system for asset recovery is bureaucratic, expensive and ineffective.

The power does not rest with people at all—civic power rests with a handful of ultra-rich private investors. We do not have freedom and equality. In reality, we do not even have a democracy.

My quest had just become bigger than giving the public the secret to finding their own financial freedom. My quest was about shifting civic power and economic control from private investors to the people. It had become about truly inspiring and empowering the people. It had become a battle for the democratic rights of citizens, meaning, you!

Back in 2008, many banks were engaged in subprime lending and packaging, selling and investing in collateralised debt obligations. This resulted in a global crisis for the banking system.

As head of investments at the world's largest bank I was striving towards living my life purpose by taking the bank in a different direction. Product managers had numerous skills and a great deal of knowledge and I was no different. Taking what could have been a very mundane career, I shifted my attention to healing a part of world grief.

Relying on my product development skill set and marketing knowledge, my team launched a sterling denominated vaccine bond. The project was responsible for immunising 130 of the world's poorest children against preventable diseases for every £1,000 invested.

Leading a small group of committed people to make something truly momentous happen, I was humbled by the results—they were awe-inspiring. The first bond buyer was the pope!

In 2009, we picked up an award for the best investment product in the world. Most importantly, according to the World Health Organisation, the bond contributed to saving the lives of five million children.

This delivered significantly against the UN Millennium Development Goals for child mortality. And just goes to show that by using our unique abilities and perspective, whilst leveraging our everyday gifted potential, ordinary people can achieve extraordinary things.

This is what I did. What can you do?

Imagine what you could achieve just by making the change.

Visualise the outcome. Create your reality. Act as though you cannot fail.

This imperative is a wake-up call (for you) to address world imbalance at a critical time in history. To be accountable for your impact upon the world, rather than waiting for (and blaming) others to take up the mantle.

After the vaccine bond, my mission was to restore trust to the least trusted industry globally—the financial services industry. An industry which over-emphasised value and under-emphasised values.

As an ambassador for transparency, I still aim (as part of a small group of committed like-minded people) to move the global economic system from imbalance to balance. This is achieved by making the system more values based.

As part of an independent, collaborative, campaigning community, we seek to restore a greater mission to an otherwise purely intellectual global economic system.

With utmost integrity and determination, the *Transparency Taskforce's* purpose is to improve trust and confidence in a broken financial services industry. All the while, avoiding an escalating fiscal crisis: the financial equivalent of a zombie apocalypse.

When it comes to human ability, we all have different strengths and weaknesses. The profile these create for us, causes each person to gravitate towards one of the four tenets of body, heart, mind and spirit. Therefore, it is easy for a person to become attached to the domain where they are strongest. This can lead to feeling *stuck*, a dis-ease and potentially addictive/destructive behaviours.

There may be an equal and opposite detachment with another domain where people are weaker in the form of intelligence used or how connected they feel to that domain. They will be driven by an aversion towards this weaker domain, which leads to avoidance and disconnection.

Both attachment and disconnection are a human dis-ease that leads to imbalance and suffering. All around us there awaits potential imbalance, as many people overweight or underweight attachment to the importance of ourselves or the importance of others. This is a major challenge in our lives and in wider society—an overwhelming cause of pain and suffering.

Personally, we witness the imbalance intellectually, physically, emotionally and spiritually. At a societal level, we witness the imbalance at an economic, ecological, humanitarian and transpersonal level.

Our thoughts, beliefs, feelings and actions must essentially tick all the boxes for ourselves and for others if we are to have fundamental stability in the world. Therefore, we need to make a habit of asking ourselves, *Do my goals and actions tick all four boxes?*

Intellectual: Based upon mind and intuition, it makes sense—it is logical, practical and rational.

Physical: When considering body and instinct, it is beneficial in terms of wealth, health and well-being—it is material, palpable, visible, real and actual.

Emotional: With heart and emotion, it feels… poignant, moving, touching, affecting, powerful, stirring, heart-rending, heart-warming, uplifting, impassioned, dramatic.

Spiritual: From the perspective of spirit and intuition, it is the best thing to do for all—it is bigger than ourselves or our lifetime. It is a legacy.

Gains in any one area will be imbalanced and temporary; these are unsustainable if they are at the expense of losses in other areas. Eventually, the entire imbalanced system will fail.

To avoid complete failure, it is essential to regularly take account and rebalance your life. To create peace, happiness and well-being for your life and the planet through the pursuit of balance.

As human beings we are four-natured—we coexist in intellectualism, materialism, emotionality and spirituality.

The first two natures relate to our outer world of intellect, instinct, physical objects and money. They are self-enhancing values. The latter two relate to our inner world of intuition, feelings, a sense of morality and meaning. These are self-transcending values.

Our rational, instinctive, emotional and intuitive impulses exist in absolute opposition to one another and paradoxically, they must coexist for each of us to live a life well lived. Through this polarity and perfect balance, we achieve the life we want and the life we deserve in a very real, tangible way.

Consider your finances and financial planning in relation to three different situations.

The Disintermediated: Less than £5,000 in savings. 60% of people.

Financial intermediaries are unlikely to service this group.

When living without value the aim must be to increase the money supply available for necessary consumption. This in turn increases well-being. The financial plan for the disintermediated is aimed at alleviating poverty and improving well-being. Their aim is to become sustainable and responsible financially.

Where a person has debt, they need to repay the debt in as short a space of time as possible; not forgetting to pay themselves first to live. The sustainably responsible know not to use debt to fund purchases, as this increases the cost two or three times.

The disintermediated live in material imbalance—the poverty of which translates to an inability to find the resources needed for meaningful projects. They must improve their financial position as a matter of urgency—they need income to be deployed on essential outgoings and satisfying creditors to preserve their well-being.

The Underserved: Between £5,000 and £100,000 in savings. 35% of people.

Financial intermediaries in general do not target this group.

When living sustainably and responsibly your aim is to maximise your well-being through optimising your benefits

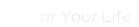

from consumption. The sustainably responsible financial plan is aimed at reaching and maintaining this comfortable standard of living throughout your lifetime. Only when you know you will not outlive your capital can you focus on the next step of meaningful projects.

Where income exceeds a responsible level of expenditure you create savings. You set aside savings for rainy days in an instant access savings account—you call this your *emergency fund*. The emergency fund should be sufficient to cover six month's expenditure.

Continuing to save, you invest in excess of your emergency fund in a *risk-balanced ethical investment portfolio* aligned to your values and beliefs. The interest and investment income you generate allows you to replace income from the job you may hate. At the tipping point, where ethical income exceeds expenditure, you find financial freedom.

The sustainably responsible continue saving beyond financial freedom to build a contingency fund. You cannot know how long you will live, although you can hedge that bet with a purchase of a lifetime annuity. You also have no clue as to what financial calamities await you. Therefore, it is useful to have money set aside for unforeseen events.

However, you do not increase your expenditure beyond what is responsible, sensible, ethical and sustainable.

The Served: Over £100,000 in savings. 5% of people.

Financial intermediaries proactively target this group.

When you are wealthy, you have excess capital. Your aim should be primarily to preserve your well-being at the comfortable, sustainably responsible expense level. Your aim is not primarily to further grow and preserve your wealth.

Do not start to spend your excess capital on frivolous things unaligned with your higher purpose. Further increases to consumption, needlessly risk reducing your well-being. For example, excess wealth may cause fear of being robbed, cause ill-health through over-consumption or stressful living through increased financial demands from others.

The excess capital should instead be deployed to increase meaning in your life: through a healthier lifestyle, living your life purpose in the service of others, improving the well-being of others and building your legacy by design.

If you do not set inspiring goals for your life, someone else will.

When bank interest rates dropped to 0.25% per annum, James asked his adviser to find him a better rate. James trusted his adviser, who in turn placed James' life savings in property-backed investments carrying a guaranteed return of 8% per annum.

For the first few years James was delighted. Then payments stopped. The firms defaulted due to an internal fraud. And the adviser closed his advice firm, declaring himself insolvent.

James lost his savings, while the adviser (who had taken up to 25% commission on the investments) lost his livelihood. The solicitor advised James that pursing a case against his adviser was not worthwhile.

Heather was delighted with her adviser. Whenever she asked him a question he responded within an hour. Her investments had grown. He took his fees out of the investment. His fee was explicit. What was not explicit was the fee others in the supply chain had taken from the investment.

More of her return was taken by the middle man than was given to Heather. Heather bore all the risk. She also didn't know how her investment performance compared to an ethical tracker fund she could have bought directly from a provider for a fraction of the price. She just knew that the value of her investment went up.

Her adviser had not disclosed the full extent of the fees taken, that promised returns are seldom delivered, the full extent of the risk taken by his client and the impact on people and planet. Yet, Heather would not tolerate a bad word said about her adviser.

Gill wanted to open an individual savings account. Her best friend's partner was an adviser. He told her for free about a direct-to-the-public investment platform where she invested £20,000 into a balanced tracker fund. She saved herself a great deal on charges and advice fees and was delighted with the performance.

James, Heather and Gill each trusted their adviser with very different outcomes.

Most people would be better off by following the direct route to investing, like Gill. If most people did this, the result would be an all-inclusive financial system that contributed to greater prosperity and better met society's needs. The vast majority of the population underserved by banks would be served. The trouble is, most people do not.

Not everyone has access to good financial advice—personal advice does not come cheap. Cheaply priced financial adviser services for low-value investment clients are unprofitable for advisers to deliver and are unsustainable. For this reason, they are uncommon.

Responsibly (higher) priced advice models seldom provide value for money for the small investor, as they absorb a disproportionate amount of the investment return. For this reason, financial advisers tend to restrict their offerings to a minority of more affluent investors.

The rationale for disintermediation is, the financial adviser must earn a reasonable standard of living. A financial adviser will pay a third of revenue in operating expenses, a third as company profit and a third as salary. To pay themselves £66,000 they would need to earn almost £200,000 in revenues annually. If they could service a maximum of 100 clients, two a week, this requires that they charge each client £2,000 per annum.

It would be indecent for advisers to extract the required going rate, of say £2,000 per annum, from each client's life savings where pots are small.

In the past the deduction was hidden in commission payments from your pot. Legislation over the past two decades has made adviser charges more transparent. This transparency serves people and it denies them access to good financial advice.

95% of the population are underserved, disintermediated and orphaned by the financial adviser community because of their limited wealth. This trend, over the past two decades, demonstrates levels of protection and savings will only decrease in future.

Surveys[5] tell us that about three-fifths of all UK adults have no savings or savings of less than £5,000 and that roughly one-third of all UK adults have no private pension. Furthermore, two-thirds of UK adults have no life insurance or other protection cover. In the UK…

- Unsecured household debt will soon reach 50% of household income.

- Credit card debt takes over twenty-five years to repay at minimum repayment levels.

- There are over 1,000 adults made redundant every day.

- There are over 4,500 debt problems reported daily to the Citizens Advice Bureau.

- Over 1,700 County Court Judgements daily.

- A property is repossessed every hour.

- There is an insolvency or bankruptcy every five minutes.

Financial struggle is on the increase.

More than half (52%) of the UK population are living on the edge financially[6]. This is a sharp increase from 35% of people who were having difficulty maintaining household bill payments when similar research was carried out in 2006.

Nearly a fifth of those surveyed would go out for the evening even if they could not afford it and 17% made non-essential purchases when they were not in a financial position to do so.

The figures are terrifying.

Living in these circumstances makes it feel as if the world has ended—and for many, the world ending seems to be the only solution. And the next generation of UK adults face greater financial challenges than the current.

They can face the start of their working careers with £50,000 of student debt. About 70% of graduates are expected never to finish repaying their loans, according to the Institute for Fiscal Studies. Instead they must make repayments for thirty years before eventually having the unpaid loan written off.

Mortgage providers will not lend to people carrying this much debt.

The next generation may struggle to step on the property ladder. It can take a further fifteen years to save up a deposit for home ownership and younger workers in the meantime face the additional burden of woefully underfunded pension pots, with the pillars of state and employers no longer able to provide.

A combination of debt, joblessness, globalisation, demographics and rising house prices is depressing the incomes and prospects of millions of young people across the developed world.

The implications of this unprecedented inequality between generations would be to witness the disappearance of the global middle class in a single generation in developed countries.

Intergenerational inequality fuels wider inequality and growing social tension because youngsters with rich parents hold an unfair advantage in early adulthood.

Our grandchildren might well face the same economic circumstances as our grandparents (or worse), as a property-less working class pay ever-increasing taxation to fund runaway levels of social security.

Where has the wealth gone?

According to Oxfam, the top 1% of the global population have as much financial wealth as the bottom 99% combined. This is where the wealth has gone—and the divide is getting worse. The rich are getting richer, whilst the poor are getting poorer.

Since the turn of the century we have witnessed an upward trend with more and more wealth being horded by the few at the expense of the many. This so-called *elite* own our media, our oil and as we have seen, our government.

They leverage the power of ownership to finance wars and maintain a degree of chaos which blindsides us—keeping our eyes firmly fixed on each other and our differences, rather than them and their criminal activity.

What drives money to the elite is our education system— teaching a club-thumping habit of memorising the constant barrage of information white noise without thinking. To obey without question, the constant indoctrination, terror generated by division and fear of punishment. Their biggest weapon by far is the banking system.

We are now being used as money slaves. We work long hours for the best part of our lives, in boring and depressing environments, not stimulated by anything creative or constructive.

Tax collectors help themselves to a big chunk of what you earn and the rest is paid directly to the bank, cutting out the wage earner (you). You then divvy out credits to the bank and big corporations. Look at the coins in the bottom of your purse to see how much you actually got paid.

Big corporations pay ridiculous amounts to CEOs and less than a living wage for the rest. Designed to keep you in limbo, without time for education, introspection or awakening to the prospect of a higher way.

When we are educated, capable of critical thinking and have higher goals, we are dangerous to the establishment. To counter this, fear is weaponised, because fear shuts down critical thinking and provokes anger.

Angry, frustrated and mindless, we conform to their desires and goals—we operate machines, keep the system running and never ask questions.

World grief in its entirety is profitable for the 1% elite. They make money from war, disease, human exploitation and the ever-increasing destruction of our planet.

At the other end of the spectrum, the world's 3.5 billion poorest adults—the war-ravaged, diseased, exploited and displaced people who make up 50% of the population—account for just 2.7% of the world's wealth.

We can end wage slavery.

We can reverse this trend with values-based economics and the principles of *Your Money or Your Life!* Your true inheritance for future generations could be the lasting legacy you create through this *paradigm*.

And it is not a question of overthrowing governments or the banking elite—this is about you being who you are. Not the money-addicted, work-crushed, brain-addled automaton of elitist design. Nor the blind beggar, chasing the illusion of wealth to the grave, but you—living your life as you.

Rich is what you have in your mind, body, heart and spirit. Not your bank account.

Remember, you can have no money to your name and still be a money addict!

Take Irene, for example.

She's 85 years of age and lives alone, vulnerable and motivated by fear. Over her lifetime, she willingly handed over the contents of her bank account to people on the other side of the globe. People she has never met, but who claim to use her money to enter the Australian lottery on her behalf.

She refers to these strangers as her *friends*.

On the rare occasions when her bank queries these strange transactions, she stuffs cash in envelopes and posts them southwards. She occasionally is teased with cash sent back, although postal workers have lost their jobs as they knew how to spot the envelopes. This practice is widespread throughout the world.

When the local post office queried the situation, Irene wrote an irate letter to bosses at postal headquarters, complaining about their conduct—it was not the business of postal workers to question her.

The scam constantly left her penniless—it always has.

Today she gets £500 per month in state pension paid to her bank and every penny is spent on the pursuit of that elusive antipodean win. They take small amounts every day, emptying her account when they can.

For years, this failed to raise a significant red flag with the bank, they just stood by and watched; levying unauthorised overdraft penalties and declined payment charges. All the while, Irene is unable to buy food or clothes. She cannot afford a hairdresser, heat her house or even meet friends for a coffee.

This is what retirement can be like. And it's terrifying!

Irene is obsessed by the opportunity to win and refuses to hear a wrong word about her *friends* when her family attempt to intervene.

"When I win, I will go and live in Switzerland." Irene smiles at the thought.

Her higher-way robbers are obvious—the Australian charlatans running the scam and the bankers who just let it happen.

Just as money addicts may have no money, love addicts can fail to find love. Control addicts may have no control. Religious addicts can possess no spirituality. You don't have to have something to be addicted to it. It is an unquenchable desire that takes hold, regardless of the reality a person lives in. The consequences are devastating—lives are destroyed.

Higher-way robbers rob you of your money, which robs you of your ability to survive. What is not so obvious at first glance is that they are robbing you of your life! People can live beyond their means and get into financial trouble. People can just as easily have means beyond their living, which is often more dangerous.

James is 75 and lives alone—he has never had a family of his own

When he was just six years old, James turned to his father and asked, "Dad, can I have one of them chickens?"

James pointed to the corner of the field.

"What would you be wanting with a chicken?" his father replied, puzzled.

"I want to sell the eggs and make some money!"

"You'd be wasting your time," James' dad replied with a shake of his head, "you'll never make any money at that!"

James was determined to prove his dad wrong; to show him what he could achieve. So, James embarked on a ruthless campaign to own a chicken, which after many weeks of cajoling and relentless pressure, succeeded. James got his chicken.

According to his plan, James sold the eggs and he never spent a penny of the money he made. He eventually had more chickens and sold increasing quantities of eggs, yet he still

or Your Life

refused to part with his hard-earned cash. He was going to show his father in no uncertain terms that he could make his fortune as an egg magnate.

James worked long hours, all day, every day. Looking to take eggs from an overstocked farmer here and there and supplying them to understocked shops and markets.

He soon earned the moniker of *The Egg Man of Wigan*.

This constituted the entirety of James' life. He never drank. Never smoked. Refused to socialise. Did not travel—never took a holiday. Never married, nor had kids. He was always too busy.

He inherited a house from his parents when they passed in the sixties and to this day, he still has all the same furniture, carpets and curtains.

"Hey Steve, see that couch there…" he chuckled, with a gesture to the sofa in his living room. "I was born on that there couch!"

He proudly supports the malicious practices of Walmart through the purchase of clothes from George at Asda. He buys his food on a Thursday evening from Tesco, from the bargain corner. A week's shopping for £2.97!

He travels a little more these days, now he has his free bus pass.

There is no television, no computer, no central heating. Just a seldom-lit, old and lonely gas fire; a reminder of the way James has lived his entire life. In his words, "I spend nothing. Never have."

James is a multimillionaire!

I first met James in 2012, as I set up my own financial advice firm after leaving the banks. He was referred to me because he had a problem with his previous financial adviser, who turned out to be a money addict (as they often are).

With the banking crisis of 2008, the central banks slashed interest rates to virtually nothing. James had all his money on deposit at his local bank and it was, "Doing nowt!"

The Independent Financial Adviser had taken all of James' savings and invested it in a falsely-titled *guarantee scheme*—unregulated property-backed securities. A million here, a million there, a million scattered around a few smaller investments.

After all, James *should not hold all his eggs in one basket!*

The IFA had taken as much as 25% in commission on what were essentially all scams! Every single last one of those investments failed. Each time the investment house claimed it was not them, it was *the market*... The property development market had failed, the asset was illiquid and they couldn't return his money.

In reality, scammers had creamed off receipts and when the pyramid scheme was starved of new investment, they would shut up shop and move on to the next scam.

The regulators did nothing to help James. The ombudsman was unable to help as the IFA had shut up shop too, without insurance. The police remained uninterested. The SFO looked the other way. Lawyers said there was nothing to be done.

This was when my conversations with James began; when I set about unmasking the higher-way robbers one by one.

James told me. "They're all at it. If I had half of your brains, I'd be at it too."

Six years later, James has recovered most of his money back through more and more people putting pressure on the

Government, regulators and the more responsible providers. Yet, this is not the worst of it.

When it comes to getting back James' life, we were less than successful.

"When you are 85 and looking back on the past ten years of your life," I enquired. "What would you have it be? What did you have? What did you do?"

"I'd do nothing. Spend nothing," James replied. "If I spent money, it would make it seem as though the last 75 years of my life has been a complete waste of time. I'll not be spending any money I can assure you."

The very first of James' higher-way robbers had devastated his life; sending a cascade of events, situations and circumstances that robbed him of life. A cascade that placed him on the lonely road towards other higher-way robbers and their deathly cries of *Stand and deliver*!

When it comes to financial fraud, so little is ever recovered, the police do not get involved, the SFO not interested, policymakers just don't care. The turnover of criminal proceeds is unbelievably high—a reported £4 billion in the UK alone each year is illegally misappropriated.

But this pales into insignificance when we consider the cases where no laws are broken. In the UK asset management industry, £80 billion to £120 billion is taken in undisclosed fees and charges from everyone's life savings. With the UK making up only 4% of the global economy, that's £2.5 trillion that goes unaccounted for globally.

The greatest bank heist of all time was achieved by Qusay Hussein, Saddam Hussein's second son. Just before the invasion of Iraq by allied forces in the Gulf War, he removed $1 billion from Iraq's Central Bank.

Banks rob us of many times this amount every year, legally.

This is why I campaign so fervently for greater transparency. And it is why we all have a responsibility to wake from our slumber. To stand up and witness with an unflinching stare, the global plundering of life and money by the bankers.

When money is stolen, so too is life. The theft of intellectual capital, the plundering of Earth's precious resources, the exploitation of humanity and the associated loss of emotional capital caused by wars.

Consider the loss of spiritual capital. Seven billion people living mundane, empty, uninspiring lives. Waiting solely for their next pay cheque, they are locked into conditioned living. A prison in which they will never achieve a legacy that lasts more than a few years beyond their lifetime.

Your Money or Your Life! Seeks to balance physical capital, intellectual capital, emotional capital and spiritual capital—it is not simply financial planning, but *life planning*.

PART FOUR

A HIGHER WAY

The economic system is not democratic.

The economic system is controlled by private owners, who are essentially bound within a paradigm, saturated by inequality. The holders of many stocks have more say than the holders of few stocks.

The City does not want you to know this, but you—along with every other individual in the world—have the power to completely change the way things are done.

Every time you spend money, you are aligning your values with those of the organisation you are spending with. You fund the values of that business, so if they finance fracking, you are supporting environmental destruction. If they invest in ethical manufacturing, you are helping eliminate sweatshops!

This also counts for investments, because you can ask the institutions who represent you to invest according to your personal values. *Every unit of currency you invest is a powerful vote for the change you wish to see in this world.*

For example, if British people invested according to their values, then over three trillion pounds would be invested sustainably and responsibly. In economic terms, trillions of pounds have the amazing potential to swiftly bring peace to the world, feed the hungry and save our planet from climate change.

Yet, this is not in the interests of those who have money and power. Banks and other financial institutions serve the rich and the rich do not profit from feeding people who are starving, tackling environmental challenges or ending war.

The rich do profit by keeping us divided—misaligned with each other and in relation to how we demonstrate our own values in the world. Yet we now have the opportunity for an extraordinary transition. We can all align our actions with our values.

Our values are those principles and qualities that matter dearly to us—our very foundations that affect how we process and perceive the world round us. How we invest our time and money speaks volumes about our values.

Knowing and striving for our own values is essential for higher-way living. Appreciating the values of others is also important, because the biases we have about others are what banks use to divide us.

When we have an accurate picture of what our fellow humans believe, we can interpret and predict how banks (et al), leverage our differences to cause fragmentation in society. We can also heal the rifts between ourselves and those who have contrasting values.

Examine this representation of values and identify where ten of your values reside. Make a note of these and then ponder where you see the values of other people in relation to your own.

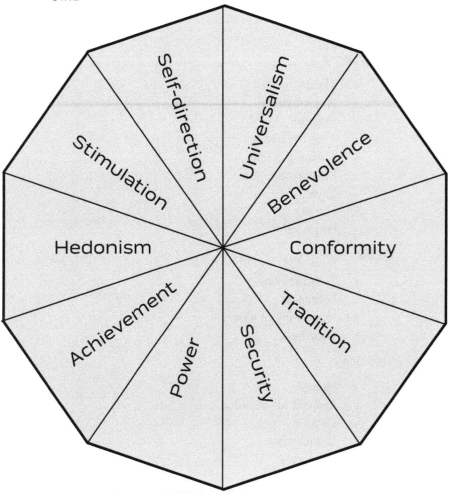

Universalism

- Protect the environment
- Unity with nature
- A world of beauty

- A world at peace
- Inner harmony
- Broadminded
- Social justice
- Equality
- Wisdom

Benevolence

- Mature love
- A spiritual life
- Helpful
- True friendship
- Meaning in Life
- Responsible
- Loyal
- Honest
- Forgiving

Conformity

- Self-discipline
- Politeness
- Honouring of elders
- Obedient

Tradition

- Humble
- Respect for tradition
- Devout
- Detachment
- Moderate
- Contentment

Security

- Healthy
- Family security
- Social order
- Clean

- Sense of Belonging
- Reciprocation of favours
- National security

Power

- Social recognition
- Wealth
- Authority
- Social power
- Control
- Preserving public image
- Fame
- Celebrity

Achievement

- Successful
- Intelligent
- Capable
- Influential
- Ambitious

Hedonism

- Pleasure
- Enjoying life
- Self-indulgent
- Physical Appearance
- Fantasy

Stimulation

- An exciting life
- Daring
- A varied life

Self-direction

- Freedom
- Curious
- Creativity
- Choosing own goals

- Privacy
- Self-respect
- Independent

A 2016 survey of one thousand, demographically representative UK citizens revealed that three out of four ordinary people placed compassionate values above selfish values.[7]

Perhaps shockingly, three out of four went on to express how they believed their fellow citizens held selfish values in greater esteem. This startling evidence reveals the extent of the manipulation—three-quarters of people who participated in the survey have compassionate values and three-quarters believed others did not!

We are more alike than we know.

Most people fail to have a clear, defined and designed vision of their path through life—they wander aimlessly and powerless. Intimidated by government and religious forces that seek to dominate and control, most are steered this way and that way; they follow a path created for them.

In the shadow cast upon this path they lose all sovereignty. They live as others expect them to live—pawns in someone else's game of chess.

This journey into darkness begins in childhood, when we are taught to place the immense power within ourselves into shadow. We start identifying more and more with the identity we are given by others. We sacrifice our power to consciously adapt for survival in the outside world—but there is a point where survival becomes control.

We are taught the limitations in which we confine ourselves for an entire lifetime, in line with socially acceptable behaviours. Schools indoctrinate us through technical and social skills, designed for a material life. Society is geared towards materialism and maintaining the status quo of dominance and control.

We adapt to the goals and desires of others. This is the way of our world.

There is no meaningful inner exploration or development for children. Children are not taught about intuition, the subconscious mind, independent thought, self-esteem, self-confidence or real inner spiritual growth. The person they have the potential to be is lost in the shadow, lost in the business of the world outside of themselves.

In Greco-Egyptian mythology, Hermes Trismegistus was a master of alchemy, astrology and theurgy (practice of rituals). He is believed to have authored the sacred texts of *Hermeticism*; the elucidation of which is *The Kybalion* (which was published in 1908 and written anonymously under a pseudonym of the *Three Initiates*).

The hermetic texts have been studied over many centuries by philosophers and scientists, such as Ralph Waldo Emerson and Isaac Newton, as well as being reworked and presented by many personal, professional and business development gurus.

The Kybalion principle of *mentalism* informs us that you are the creator of your own reality through thought. Whether conscious or unconscious, you create your truth.

Even when, at a conscious level you have the appearance of being still, at a subconscious level the pendulum of creation is still swinging. You are never truly standing still—nothing rests—you are always creating, forever in the rhythm of the natural cycle from creation to manifestation. Whether you know it or not.

At any given point in the creative cycle, one of your types of intelligence is in the driving seat of thinking. Whether this is mind, body, heart or spirit (IQ, PQ, EQ or SQ), the driving force of that intelligence will take us far in one direction until we change drivers.

Of course, this is imbalanced and to achieve anything in a harmonious or balanced way, we must keep reviewing and consciously swapping our drivers. By applying the best intelligence for the task at hand, with foresight and design, we eventually manifest the changes we seek.

To take the unreal, imaginary or visionary and to make it real, we need all four aspects of our whole being. This is the cycle of creation to manifestation. If a person fails to change drivers, they risk swinging back and forth, doomed to repeat and repeat like a pendulum, under the *principle of rhythm*.

The principal of neutralisation allows us to continue the cycle—traversing a higher way—to avoid the return swing of the pendulum. By denying the power or influence of the return swing over us, we neutralise it and evolve by moving towards a definite result.

When we apply the principles of *The Kybalion* to life, we notice a constant imbalance between meaning and money. It is a cycle of imbalance, from one bumpy moment to the next.

This makes life challenging, because in one moment we attach too much attention to money at the expense of meaning, at the next the pendulum swings and we attach too much focus to meaning at the expense of money.

Your aim is to hold the balance between meaning and money; to smooth out the bumps and evolve towards a deeper sense

of equilibrium. As you gradually diminish life's imbalance, you will learn profound lessons in the repeated cycles of life. You literally get better at it as you go along!

Learning through the cycles of life, you consistently spiral upwards from the lower way to the higher way. And from that higher way, you can navigate the fraught and tangled path of the lower way with a greater insight. Understanding how those who attempt to solve the problems of the lower way, from the lower-way perspective, will enable you to see the challenges within yourself.

Imagine your subconscious mind to be an expansive wilderness of grasslands, pine forest, mountain ranges, rivers, canyons and lakes. Your conscious awareness is but a small meadow. In this meadow, two wolves sit. They are always at war with each other.

The wolves are of equal weight and have two alternating primal states of being. When it is cloudy and overcast the wolves are receptive, yielding, weak, passive and retreat. When it is sunny and bright both wolves are creative, firm, strong, active and advance.

One wolf, however, is fearful, greedy and hateful. The other is brave, kind and loving.

Stop and think about it. Which wolf wins the fight?

The one you feed.

Food is the cause, winning the effect. What you feed your conscious mind has results that not only affect you consciously, but also impact your subconscious. Your truth, your *reality* is a manifestation of your thinking—how your consciousness sits between your subconscious resources and superconscious potential.

Consciousness is what we operate with during our daily activities and waking hours. It represents around 0.1% to 2% of our experience and consists of processing the package, filtered information we receive from the outside world and internal experience.

The subconscious records everything: every activity we engage in, our thoughts about those activities, our likes and dislikes about what we encounter each day. It is a primal, potent force and has a tremendous influence on how we think and act when in a conscious state.

The superconscious encompasses a level of awareness that experiences both material reality and beyond. The superconscious thoughts are not derived from any individual person—they do not belong to us—but instead comprise part of a collective consciousness.

Universally available to those who are aware of this degree of thought, it is a powerful, transpersonal force that we access through our intuition. The superconscious is how some people predict trends, whilst others arrive at the same inspiration, conclusion or breakthrough completely independently (and on opposite sides of the globe).

Most people are not conscious of their path of purpose, mission or legacy. Purpose is born from superconscious into subconscious, yet, when using meaningful intent we can access purpose in a conscious way.

It is important to question everything you accept and believe to be true, question childhood lessons and what you have blindly accepted throughout your life. Then to compare the questions and answers with your values—noticing any discrepancies.

You need to know your values, the true meaning of these values and their purpose in your life. This is the only way to live true to yourself and not as others expect you to live. Knowing your values will activate you. It motivates you. It moves you to get up in the morning, sustains you when times get tough, serves as a compass if you stray way off course. It inspires in lasting, lifelong ways.

When people blindly chase money to the grave, they miss the deeper meaning in life; they forget to feed their hearts and spirit. When people chase meaning to the grave, it may be an earlier grave through lack of money. They forget to feed the physical body and the intellectual mind.

Life is so much easier when you decide on a meaningful life, your values and your very purpose; then put in place the actions and money to achieve it.

Reflect upon the earth for one moment. Ponder all the beauty of the earth. Explore how rare it is that it supports life. Your life. Earth is unique in that it is the only planet we know of that has intelligent life upon it.

Many treat the earth as they would a mirror. They stand in one place and look at their reflection in another place. However, the earth is not a reflection of you—the earth is you! And you are the earth.

You were not dropped here from an alien spacecraft… you were born here and you will die here. And in every moment, in between, your body is made up of the earth.

The nutrients you need to survive exist, grow and are sustained by the earth. The water in your body was, last month in the ocean, the clouds, flowing through somebody else. The air in your lungs was made by plants and is the same breath of all people. You are totally dependent on Earth for your very survival.

The love you possess for yourself and your family is love for the earth—for they are all the same. When you commit to making a change in your life that cares for Earth, you make that change available for the whole planet.

Ponder the piece of the world's grief you are meant to fix. Consider your interconnectedness with others. Your own personal growth can ripple through and affect the growth of the whole planet.

You are not born to heal *all* world grief, just some aspect of it. This may be an aspect you see in the world or one you see in yourself (possibly both). Explore how you might help the human family to grow and help the planet to heal.

For some it is an impossible task. For others it is of no consequence. Most people would view this as a daunting prospect. The sheer immensity of solving the Earth's problems prevents many people from beginning. Yet, we each can make changes in ourselves to make the world better.

You were born to heal the part of world grief associated with your unique values and talent. Others were born to heal the other problems. Most people do not know where to start. Most people do not take the first step. When the first step remains untaken, world grief lingers, the human family remains preoccupied with the mundane and the devastation of the planet continues.

Most people do not know how to transition from creation to manifestation. Some may create ideas, fewer communicate their creation to others, fewer still ground the idea with a plan of action, hardly anybody manages and mobilises resources to deliver an outcome.

So, only those dedicated enough, resilient enough and accountable for themselves enough manifest their creations.

For others, the cycle begins well then grinds to a staggering and irrevocable halt.

Failing to make the world better through living in it, leads to a deathbed of regrets and being forgotten with the passage of time. The legacy of most is a mossy tombstone, a rosebush or a crumbling obituary.

When you know how to complete the cycle from creation to manifestation—when you can make intangible ideas and imaginings into real, physical reality—you change the world.

We all experience moments of happiness and sadness in life. Most people mistakenly pursue the dream of permanent happiness through desires and attachment, at the expense of a lasting contentment.

Few people have the wherewithal to know the difference between the elusive concept of happiness we are told to strive for and true, lasting contentment. Few people experience unwavering contentment when they move from joy to times of sorrow.

By hunting the illusion of permanent happiness, people are fooled by temporary satisfaction and they are devastated by its inevitable loss. Destroyed by their own desire for happiness when life deals them moments of grief, they end up suffering ongoing loss, broken and in bits.

Contentment is not about making do or settling for less. It is the difference between feeling a sense of real achievement, nourishment and serenity by just being on your path (rather than craving the exhilaration of reaching a mythical destination that is not even on your path).

Contentment comes for each of us when it is derived from creating a lasting legacy.

It would not occur to most people to knowingly create a lasting legacy—to create something that will still be in the world long after they are gone. Yet all around us are the legacies created by those who have long since departed.

Our world is full of them—they are our heritage. And, although we are surrounded by them, people usually take them for granted. Recognising the value of our shared heritage will give you the foundations and resources you need to begin your own journey towards a lasting legacy.

When people hold inaccurate beliefs about other's values, they feel significantly less inclined to get involved in society—joining meetings, voting, volunteering and contributing in other ways.

They also report greater social alienation, feeling diminished responsibility for their communities and are less likely to feel they fit in with wider society. That is, relative to citizens who have greater accuracy in their perception of the real consensus.

Three-quarters of us are values based, but think that three-quarters are not.

They do nothing and say nothing about their self-transcending beliefs, driven by the misguided fear of being in a minority; of standing out from the crowd. They fail to walk their talk or live an authentic life—even when, by achieving a higher way we are better off cerebrally, physically, emotionally and spiritually.

They think living a valuable life is abnormal. So they do nothing.

Perception matters.

The decision makers in positions of power are those with lower concern about social and environmental issues, who are more concerned with wealth, recognition, popularity and ambition.

They get the votes, because they have designed a world where people vote for them.

Politicians, the press, corporate bosses, bankers are those in power who would encourage society to forget self-transcending values and instead, promote self-enhancing values. They create imbalance in society by feeding false perceptions. Because this feeds votes.

A movement towards values is a movement away from over-materialistic tendencies.

Instead of separation, we find togetherness. Instead of manipulation, we find greater sovereignty. Instead of being controlled, we find self-governing control and empowerment. A movement away from fear is a movement towards greater freedom, love, joy and an ease of living.

The power to change things has always rested within you. If we can each find the power within ourselves to transform from imbalance to balance, we can become the change we wish to see in the world.

Our television and newspapers thwart original thinking.

The media publish the agenda of those in power; they publish to the perceptions of popular opinion, rather than the truth. We are fed a constant diet of survival, arrive on time, be silent, go to work, fit in with society, struggle to make ends meet, low-cost over value-based purchases, work hard, strive to be happy, live when you've retired, win the lottery.

A self-fulfilling prophecy: we are taught to fear death by fearing to live. We are held to unachievable beauty standards and then made to feel displeasure at ourselves because we do not look that way.

So, we eat to feel better and drown out the emotion with TV; eventually leading a sedentary, obese life. Those in power want us to be safe, harmless, inactive, productive cattle, fattened up to feed their hunger for more.

We need to live in the world consciously and not get lost in it. Follow your own purpose. Have your own mission. Live to your own rules. Play your own game. Design your own legacy.

In Japan there is a budgeting journal called *Kakebo*. It is conscious money, financial tidiness, declutter and minimalism. At the beginning of the month you decide how much to save and what to do. You note your weekly spending. Tally up. It makes improving your life a habit.

You must become conscious of how money *actually* comes and goes in your life, rather than how you *think* it comes and goes. Before we develop wealth in mind, body, heart and spirit we must first develop integrity in our wallets and purses. Money mindfulness, if you will.

How closely have you kept track of how the money flows in and out of your life this month?

Itemise every penny you earn and spend. Keep a journal, like the *Kakebo*. Categorise. Sub-categorise your categories. Then ask, *Have I aligned my earnings and spending with my values this month? Have I voted with my money for the world I want to live in?*

If you have not aligned your money with your purpose statement, then you know what you must do. You must change your habits.

Again, perceptions matter!

List your perceptions. Go through them. Check that they align with the reality you want to live.

Take definite, practical and consistent action to release false perceptions with conscious intention. Reprogramme your subconscious mind by replacing false perceptions with facts.

Life is not a competition to accumulate wealth, nor an attempt to satisfy the never-satiated appetite of some Hungry Ghost. It is not a fast-trading property game to become an economic elite with obscene passive income through rents whilst bankrupting others. Life is not a period of hermitage, hidden away in caves to journey back to Divine Source or Great Nature.

Life is a collaboration of people on this planet Earth who hold within themselves passion and purpose and who wish to walk the middle path. Where we each take immense pleasure from the virtues of friendship, loving kindness and generosity and each seek to manifest through intelligence, industry and science, feelings and values.

It is one thing to talk about the need to bring together meaning and money in our lives and quite another to set about doing it. Execution is paramount—if humankind has struggled for 10,000 years with the marriage of meaning and money, who is to say that we will not struggle for the next 10,000 years?

In many Eastern traditions, your journey of personal transformation is born out of creation. It begins with intuition and the spark of a creative idea—your potential. It then takes you on a journey, following a path from creation to manifestation, culminating in a lasting legacy.

The cycle, from creation to manifestation and beyond, takes you through four simple paths in the GAME Plan: Goals, Actions, Means and Execution. The four paths (Creation, Communication, Transaction and Manifestation), engage every form of intelligence (SQ, EQ, PQ and IQ) in a balanced and relational way.

or Your Life

Goals: Path of Creation

Actions: Path of Communication

Means: Path of Transaction

Execution: Path of Manifestation

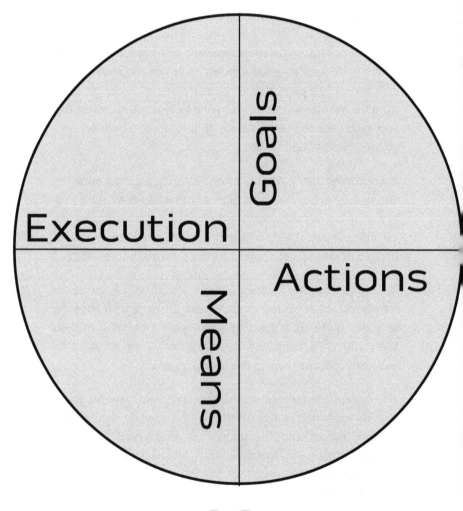

GOALS

When walking the Path of Creation, through the *Goals* quadrant, you imagine, define and connect with your ideal life: applying the currency of all four personal tenets.

This journey from North to East moves you from creation to sharing the concept, through interaction with others: communication. We start with beliefs and move round to feelings—essentially developing a purpose statement and testing it in the world.

Some people do not have goals. Perhaps they have only formulated incomplete or insignificant goals. For them, this is equivalent to leaving port in a boat without knowing the destination. When a person's goals are incomplete, they are not inspired on their journey and the eventual destination holds only disappointment.

Insignificant goals will not offer personal growth and fulfilment—they possess little or no benefit to anyone, least of all the person with them. The more significant a goal—the greater the impact on the world—the more rewards it offers.

Goals must be complete, significant and inspiring.

To help you decipher worthwhile goals, complete the series of questions below. Your answers offer an insight into where your goals can be found. When answering, avoid judgement and the temptation to judge the goals. Simply observe them.

Choose a setting for this exercise: one that maximises comfort and minimises distraction. Prepare yourself by ensuring you have a clear and calm headspace—use breathing exercises to quieten your thoughts and become present in the moment. Have a pen and blank journal to hand for making notes.

Notice the feelings that emerge as you answer each question. And be patient… The most profound answers may take their time in coming. Defer consideration of all obstacles until the Actions stage—you need to be inspired before gathering the strength and tenacity to tackle obstacles.

Initially, you may find this exercise is dominated by the loud voice of conditioned thinking. This voice speaks from a place that is misguided and will have insufficient impact to truly inspire you. Keep answering and making notes until a quieter, softer voice takes over.

- What are your values?

- Describe what you are good at—what are your skills and talents?

- What can you do that nine out of ten people cannot do? What puts you in the top 10% of your peers?

- What would an ideal life be for you?

- If you sold your possessions and now held a big bag of cash, what would you spend it on? Would you buy exactly the same things again?

- What would you do if you won the lottery?

- Your doctor explains you only have five years to live. What would you do with your remaining time on Earth?

- Your doctor lets you know that you will die within the next twenty-four hours. What did you not get to do and who did you not get to be?

- How would you solve the world's most pressing problems? What would be your lasting legacy?

EXERCISE

Imagine in a few years from now—set a specific date—you have achieved everything you desire: a perfect life.

Write down what this looks like, what you have (possess), how you feel, how your mindset is different and what effect this has on your experience of life. Pay particular attention to where you feel emotion as these are the most significant responses.

Look back over your life acknowledging your achievements and reflect on the journey to this perfect life.

What were the successes?

What obstacles did you overcome?

What were the inspired actions that made a powerful difference to your life?

Write down the answers to these questions.

Create your purpose statement (no more than two paragraphs). This uses specific examples of your successes, tactics to overcome obstacles and the inspired actions you took to get from *here* to your *perfect life*.

Then read your statement aloud, noting anything that is missing, seems out of place or deeply moves you. Strengthen your statement by adapting it with these insights.

Come back to your purpose statement regularly. Read it aloud, truly connect with it and evolve it over time. It is a living document that grows as you do.

ACTIONS

So far you have created an inspiring narrative for moving beyond conditioned limitation and being the best you can possibly be, living with purpose and creating a lasting legacy.

In the actions phase you take your *purpose statement* and give it a reality check. This is a grounding exercise to create practical solutions, because if you do not know how to overcome obstacles, then your goals are just a dream.

Share your purpose statement with a person you trust. This is called *socialising your goals*—you are not asking them to change or critique your goals, you are simply sharing them with somebody else.

You now take the purpose statement and compare it to the physical reality of your environment. This process is rather like a negotiation between your vision and your reality. This is an instinctual task—not an intellectual one. You are going with your gut to appreciate what needs to change in your reality for it to be more like your vision.

You are seeking to ground your purpose statement with action steps and by identifying obstacles to achieving your goals. If you become confused or lose focus, return to your purpose statement and hold the vision, not the reality.

The space between a vision for the future and the current reality is known as *creative tension*. Creative tension exacts a force upon your vision, drawing it back to reality, whilst also acting on reality to move it towards your vision.

We are trained to habitually negate our vision in favour of the current reality—it is more comfortable that way. To reach your goals, however, you must hold the vision. No matter how uncomfortable it becomes. Returning to your purpose statement will help remind you of your anchor—the vision, not the reality.

The action steps you develop here are your *action plan*.

In the Action quadrant, the path takes you from socialising your goals by communication, to grounding them: making them realistic and achievable in physical reality. Again, you do this by making your reality match your vision, not dumbing down your vision to match reality!

It is here, higher-way robbers will make themselves known—seeking to rob you of your goals. They wear masks to conceal their identity—beneath the mask, we find low self-esteem, low self-respect, self-punishment, ignorance, forgetfulness, an uncaring nature, irresponsible action, pain, being controlled by others, disempowerment, misinformation, lack of trust and self-trust, struggle, fear, numbness, laziness, loss... the list goes on.

Before contemplating obstacles and higher-way robbers, check to see if anything has changed since Goals. If something urgent has arisen, you either deal with it or park it for later.

When it comes to countering robbers, form a plan that is tougher than the robber you meet. As each robber presents themselves, add to your plan an action that will overcome them—seeking to move past them, whilst also seeking strategies to trigger if you are halted at any point.

Use past situations and events to appreciate what has happened in the past, when you met this robber. Then decide what you will do to stop that from repeating itself, if you end up in the same place again.

Keep replaying your purpose statement to check it is complete and to identify any areas that are missing. Regularly ask yourself, *What could possibly stop me from achieving my goal?*

Here come the higher-way robbers!

List the obstacles one by one. Each time you listen and ask, *Is there anything else?*

As your obstacles tell you to *stand and deliver* you will find your vision moving towards your current reality. Only intervene when you sense the situation becoming critical. At this point, go back to your purpose statement and remind yourself of your goals.

When you have a complete list of obstacles, address each in turn. Observe your mood and how that robber affects you, then jot this down in relation to that obstacle.

Your solutions come from within. Start to identify these solutions to each obstacle in turn and list them in your journal as a counter to each robber. Continue to ask, *Is there anything else?*

For every solution, create a list of actions you can take to make that solution a reality—this is your high-level action plan. With this in place, you will be able to ask yourself if your purpose statement is now achievable.

Start taking the first small steps from your action plan.

By the end of *Actions* you should have: a clear set of inspiring goals contained in the purpose statement, a high-level action plan for overcoming obstacles, confidence that your purpose is realistic and achievable, identified the first step to achieving your goals.

MEANS

You are now in a position to turn actions into a usable financial model. This is stress tested numerically to define a realistic strategy and timescale for implementation. Through in-depth analysis and modelling, you achieve manageable solutions through a financially literate life plan.

Many people attempt to fulfil their goals without a financial plan. Not knowing the numbers can result in an absence of indicators when you are no longer on track. Many a best-laid plan can crash and burn on the battlefield of cash flow.

Your Means journey takes you from actions to thoughts, from instinct to intellect.

Money can be exchanged for any tangible objects in the physical world—that is the purpose of money. If you had an unlimited supply of money, you could exchange it for any tangible object you desire—that's the power of money.

Despite a common misconception, money in truth is a magical concept. Wave a magic wand and it can be transformed into any object you desire almost instantly. Almost any object can be delivered to your doorstep in twenty-four hours through the exchange of money. Money is crucial—you depend on it for your day-to-day survival. It has great power for you and *over* you.

Money is the number one, most sought-after concept in the modern world, but whilst it remains a means to an end, it is not an end in itself. There must always be one final exchange for money to be of any value. Otherwise you are left with a pile of coins, paper notes or blips on a computer screen that serve no useful purpose and have no real value in themselves.

What is the end you desire?

If the end is a life well lived, the money is how you get there (in the physical world at least). If you forget for one moment about the best things in life being free, money buys you virtually anything—it buys you a wonderful life.

Or, does it? How important are things which come free of charge?

Ponder what you believe about wealth, capital and being rich.

Now, focus upon the four types of wealth: physical capital, intellectual capital, emotional capital and spiritual capital. *Rich* is not simply what you think you have squirrelled away in your bank account, it is also what you have secured in your mind, body, heart and spirit.

Being financially wealthy cannot buy love, truth, time, peace, talent, manners, true friends, understanding, wisdom, acceptance, so on and so forth. It costs nothing to be a decent human being, so can money buy you a decent character?

Do most financial plans aim to deliver more blips on the screen of your mobile or do they aim to deliver happiness?

What is missing from most financial plans is *you*!

You are not your money! And your happiness is not in the possession of money.

The antidote to this ubiquitous challenge is a holistic wealth management programme—one that seeks to optimise all four capitals and enable you to develop fluency in the language of all four tenets.

When you invest your lifetime accumulating and balancing resources for every dimension of yourself, you achieve greater well-being in every aspect of your life and your world.

If the purpose of the financial service industry was to deliver holistic well-being instead of wealth, what would the world be like?

Compare and contrast a holistic financial plan, to a programme restricted to only money: a plan focused on a single fraction of your entire life and world. The recommendation of this plan diminishes your entire reason for living to the filling of your pockets with a worthless proxy—a facsimile that you may exchange for survival and the pursuit of satisfying unquenchable desires for things.

Staying alive and collecting paraphernalia. Attempting to feed the monkey-driven desires of your mammalian brain: the Hungry Ghost. Neglecting the needs of your human heart and greater purpose—the most lasting testament to your ever having lived.

Why is it the world's wealthiest economies are not the happiest[8]?

Why is it they report growing health problems, such as obesity, opioid epidemics and depression?

Why do we have single-purpose financial plans aimed at wealth creation and economic growth, for complex multifaceted beings who really seek greater well-being and happiness?

The world's happiest and most sought-after places to live (mostly located on the Northern European continent) care more about physical well-being (healthcare, low-crime rates, etc.), emotional connection (social reforms, relationship equality, etc.), intellectual progress (human rights laws, education, etc.) and even spiritual concepts (nations that look to the future and change, etc.).

Yet, these countries do not achieve this in a state of financial poverty—indeed they all have solid economic foundations. These foundations grow out of each nation's attitude to holistic wealth, rather than simply striving to be rich in pocket!

A life plan is closer to what makes us truly human: serving us as living people, rather than serving the money that makes others our masters. So, why have all your financial plans until now looked after your monetary needs only?

Saving for a rainy day. Saving for your retirement. Insuring for your death or ill-health. Some catastrophe happens, this pot of money appears from which you can meet all your physical needs. Problem solved!

Do your plans include the well-being that can delay the inevitable for the greatest time possible?

Goals and Action are a vision of your ideal, multifaceted life. Grounded in practical actions, your plan now required the Means to make it real. These materials and resources build a financial architecture—the foundations at your feet.

You create money in the world to support those actions without compromising your well-being and happiness. With appropriate positioning, your holistic financial plan (Life Plan) will encapsulate your potential needs for mental, physical, emotional and spiritual well-being.

When you are working at the Means stage you initially check to ascertain if anything has changed for you since the Actions stage. If any *urgent* needs have cropped up, you will deal with these or park them for later.

Most financial advisers start the advice process with money.

The financial advisers have been schooled in the old ways of planning. The approach was only relevant before the UK regulator banned commission on investment products in 2013—a step taken to rid the market of commission hungry sales people!

Lessons learnt from a time when the best advisers were those who sold the most product. From a time when the financial industry became the least trusted industry. Still, the words have changed, the sales process has not. *Commission* was replaced by the words *contingent adviser charges*.

Through successful lobbying of government and regulators by large product providers and distributors, the practices adopted to sell more product were allowed to remain. The wolf was simply permitted to dress in sheep's clothing!

The banks and regulators tell advisers what the client *needs* are (more product). And they are told to stick to it or else face the consequences. Again, the needs are not real needs. Just problems perpetrated by the banks to which the suggested needs are product solutions.

A financial plan centred here builds a life around the money—locking the client into a life with little meaning. They are handcuffed to the treadmill of work existence, in a job that fails to make them happy. They are resigned to a fate of chasing money to the grave.

If a person wants to escape this life mid-career, the last thing they need is for their savings to be locked into a pension plan until their retirement!

You have the power to insist your adviser starts with your life, rather than the money.

Advisers can be charming and persuasive, causing a person to feel powerless when wanting to question the adviser's approach. Many lack the courage to demand what they want, but

the average length of time a financial adviser listens to the customer before pulling out a financial brochure is just eighty-two seconds!

That is nowhere near long enough to get to know about your life. Because you know far more about your life than any adviser can in just over a minute, you need to be assertive. And, you are footing the bill at this banquet!

You have already been introduced to the international standard for the conventional financial planning process (ISO 22222) which was designed by bankers and is observed by advisers around the world. It starts with the brochure, skips the life and heads straight for the money. It is as follows:

1. Establish and define the customer and adviser relationship.

2. Gather customer data and determine financial goals and expectations.

3. Analyse and evaluate the customer's financial status.

4. Develop and present the financial plan.

5. Implement the financial planning recommendations.

6. Monitor the financial plan and the financial planning relationship.

The adviser following the internationally accepted best practice begins by pulling out a brochure, their terms and conditions. The data gathering is entirely focused on the Means. It is totally financial, without any basis or grounding in what purpose those finances are for.

The suitability report reads, "I identified a shortfall in retirement so I recommended a pension."

This serves the dual purpose of covering the adviser's back whilst also selling product. Therefore, the customer is locked into the treadmill of work existence from age 16 to 66 (50 years), gambling they can buy their freedom later (the last 16 years).

So, what the industry defines as *best practice* omits the life plan! Not *best practice* by any standards. With the customer's life goals and actions missing from almost all financial plans, the outcome is a lifetime cash flow forecast which locks the customer into a cycle of accumulation throughout work life and decumulation of financial wealth in retirement.

Such an adviser knows the outer world of the client and knows nothing of who they are behind the veneer. The plan produces savings for a rainy day and a pot of cash emerges from the plan as if that is all that mattered to the client and their family.

Physical objects can be bought with cash under the conventional financial plan and missing from the plan is everything else. Your purpose is to evolve fully and wholly—mentally, physically, emotionally and spiritually—to be literate in every tenet of yourself and your life.

Under the standard international plan, the client is set to accumulate and protect as much wealth as possible during their working life. They are chasing *more money* throughout their working life on a metaphorical roulette wheel.

One substantial risk overlooked in many financial plans—the recommendations are unsuitable from a risk perspective for most people!

At their point of retirement, from uninspiring mundane work, the client crystallises their funds. That is, they move from accumulation to decumulation at age 66, 67 or 68. They plan to die before their capital is exhausted.

95% of the population are in for a shock when they discover the financial reality—they must compromise their standard of living when they retire. Most people do not check the figures until it is too late. According to the Office for National Statistics, 95% of the population hold less than £100,000 in investable assets. All this amount will do is deprive the pensioner of means-tested benefits in the last 16 years of their life.

The challenge posed here is, does anyone—of the 5% or 95%—truly get to live their life in the broader sense?

At the end of life, only a few have succession plans—passing on their remaining financial capital as an inheritance for others. Another pot of cash. This time for someone else. As if that is all that matters to the beneficiary!

Throughout the journey, people seek to preserve their wealth with insurance. They live in a perpetual state of panic, fearful of losing their wealth and paying to protect it. Most forget their bigger vision and greater purpose as they become embroiled in financial terror and a lifelong struggle for financial survival.

Advisers schooled in the old ways adhere rigidly to a system, based upon a one-size-fits-all needs analysis model. This delivers optimal profits to bankers and the taxman, not for you.

The way we use money throughout our lifetime has five distinct actions or *elements*.

- We accumulate wealth during our working life.

- We crystallise wealth at our retirement.

- We decumulate wealth during our retirement.

- We pass on wealth on death, this is succession.

- We preserve and protect wealth throughout our lifetime, this is protection.

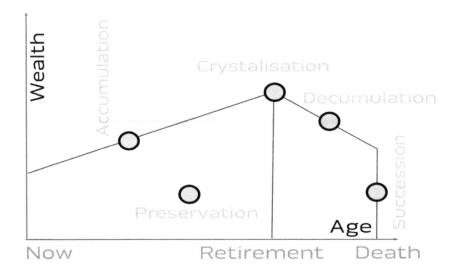

Bankers use these elements to specify the priority given to products, which affects the adviser's recommendation before you have said a single word. This is known as PRISM.

Protection

Retirement

Investments

Savings

Mortgages (this can move up or down depending on circumstances)

So, before recommending use of disposable income for a pension product, the adviser must first justify why they have not sold protection. It is strangely apt, the higher priority products are the most profitable for the banks.

When you better appreciate the relationships of the five elements you gain a greater insight into how the financial elements best work for you. As each element interacts with the others, cycles are formed.

To grasp a better understanding of Elemental Wealth, it helps to share a common language around the five elements and the three cycles these elements form. Literacy in this language will enable you to completely redefine wealth: away from how the banks want you to believe and towards you own ideals.

We must first redefine our understanding of the five elements, taking the traditional meaning and converting this to a healthier appreciation of each.

- Accumulation—the acquisition of money (metal)

- Decumulation—the spending or investment of money (wood)

- Preservation—to strengthen or enhance the current activity around money, e.g., accumulation, decumulation, etc. (earth)

- Succession—the application of money into a legacy of some kind (water)

- Crystallisation—when we transform money, things and other forms of wealth (fire)

These five elements interrelate into three cycles, which are:

- Productive

- Exhaustive

- Destructive

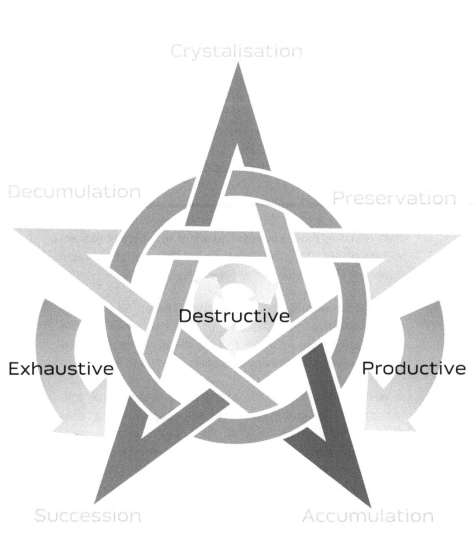

In the productive cycle we grow in holistic wealth; nurturing the four tenets by leveraging the intelligence of mind, body, heart and spirit to be fully literate in all aspects of life.

For instance, we use decumulation to crystallise money into the preservation of wealth; enabling temporary stability and confidence in your resources. A productive cycle enables us to

or Your Life

use preservation, to accumulate further and develop a greater, longer-lasting legacy, be this financial or otherwise.

However, when people are gripped by an exhaustive cycle, they diminish each element through the choices they make and behaviours they demonstrate. Accumulation only serves preservation of money until retirement, when a pension crystallises into rapid decumulation and possibly a small inheritance.

They seek to protect their finances and prevent themselves from spending money in ways that are of true benefit to them and the planet. This is problematic when they need to invest in furthering their life mission or greater legacy.

Basically, the existing financial industry is based on the ethos of an exhaustive cycle: shackling us to the treadmill of a life accumulating from 16 to 66, to feed the banks, in the vague hope of a secure and happy end of life from 66 to 82.

A destructive cycle results in a gradual implosion of self-entitlement, self-gratification and self-obsession. The core dynamic here is annihilation: the need for succession, destroying preservation (giving at the expense of one's own essential needs), accumulating only to decumulate (living from pay cheque to pay cheque, whilst struggling with poverty).

This harmful approach locks people into a central dynamic that obsesses us to the point of mutual destruction of all five elements. It leads to money stuffed in mattresses, destitution in middle age and an empty death at the end of a worthless life.

We are indoctrinated into this mode in early life from 0 to 16 and most never escape from it. Locked into self-destruction and the devouring of our planet's resources, we shelter from the pain by locking our gaze inwards. A cold, lonely death stare into our own misery and hunger.

Our productive cycle is focused upon an altruistic sharing for the benefits of all. The more we keep for ourselves the less we give to others and this leads to profit over people, planet and purpose.

The archaic attitude of the exhaustive cycle, driven by governments and banks, is to spend a life accumulating through working, combined with savings and investments. This would be a person's life through to retiring in old age, where the decumulation would kick in.

Often the exhaustive descends into the destructive with many pensioners living frugal lives, denying themselves for the fragile promise of leaving a financial legacy. True altruism and lasting legacy are distorted into selfishness-by-proxy... money for family to fight over as the only testament to a life lived.

As your life becomes values driven, the five elements constantly work on your finances as a productive cycle throughout your lifetime. You replace the old teachings with a life of repeated accumulation and decumulation, with regular succession created throughout your lifetime.

There are repeated crystallisation events as you reinvent yourself and regularly press the reset button. You will do what you can to preserve wealth, but at the same time you take measured risks for your own personal growth and development.

There will be times in your life where you are creating values, not *value*. For example, you may study or travel right in the middle of your working life if this fits your purpose.

The five elements continually consume and grow from one another creating values and diminishing value (and vice versa).

Many struggle with life because of insufficient physical capital or money, resulting in widespread financial poverty. Lack of money impacts our physical and essential safety needs: food, water, shelter, clothes and health. It impacts our personal world and creates fear for our very survival. It's terrifying at a physiological level to know we are not surviving because of a lack in the basics.

Wherever there is an absence of capital we should always seek to restore it—to achieve balance. When playing *Your Money or Your Life!*, there are several steps you can take to fix the situation. Society has conditioned you over the years to fixate on money and these thoughts do not serve you well—they are the cause of the problem!

As a human conception, money is just a fiction of the mind. As such, it is easy for banks and other financial organisations to manipulate what you think about money for their own gains. You are not your money—you have the ability to think differently about money when you appreciate the difference between you, your money and how those in power confuse the two (and want you to do the same).

When it comes to the Means for Acting on our Goals, we need to move past exhaustive and destructive cycles as these negate the GAME Plan. In the game of *Your Money or Your Life!* these cycles place higher-way robbers on your path… robbers who demand you "Stand and deliver!"

By filtering commonly-held beliefs and attitudes through the elemental system, we highlight the ambushes people regularly fall into. These innocent beliefs feed addiction, ease pain and provide transient relief.

Innocent beliefs are *blind spots* people hold about money. They are long-held, conditioned thoughts that niggle away in the back of the mind—those interrupting little mantras you repeat to yourself as a money rule.

If you are thinking about money a lot—if it keeps you awake at night or if it enters your mind at opportune, but unrelated moments—then you have an unhealthy attachment to it. You're a money addict! And you need to let go of those unhealthy thoughts.

An innocent belief is, for instance, the notion that winning the lottery is a productive and viable way of having a better life. When we run the process of buying a lottery ticket through the elemental system we appreciate how initially the process is productive.

The act of purchasing a ticket involves decumulation for the buyer. The handing over the ticket is a form of crystallisation—a transformation of money into a token of entry into the competition. However, this crystallisation is not aimed upon preservation of wealth (productive cycle)—it seeks to accumulate wealth (destructive cycle).

Crystalisation

Decumulation

Preservation

Succession

Accumulation

or Your Life

Buying lottery tickets weekly (or with greater frequency) is a direct relationship between crystallisation and accumulation, which usually leads to decumulation over many years. And even if a person does hit the jackpot, they usually spend it (decumulate) very quickly.

When building an *investment portfolio* (crystallisation into preservation), we seek to profit from that investment (accumulation). Wherever there are gains there are corresponding losses, which create a destructive cycle between accumulation and decumulation.

To alleviate this cycle, focus on the legacy (succession) of your accumulation. Consider how ethical your portfolio is—when you are benefitting people, planet and purpose, you maintain a productive cycle. Making money to spend money without regard for others will keep you a hostage of the financial industry.

Crystalisation

Decumulation

Preservation

Succession

Accumulation

Ponder your beliefs around money and write these down.

Examples of these could be:

- Greater wealth makes you happier

- Assets are low-risk or high-risk

- If you have the chance to make a quick buck, do it!

- Property ownership is the key to wealth

Or maybe some common clichés around money and finances:

- Money is the root of all evil

- If you look after the pennies, the pounds will look after themselves

- Money is power

- Speculate to accumulate

- Beggars can't be choosers

- A penny saved is a penny earned

Ask, *Do these beliefs serve you?*

Do they align with the reality you want to create in your life?

Are they aligned with the life you want to live or are they higher-way robbers?

Note those which limit you. Go deeper than a cursory nod of the head—take a few days to really think about how these beliefs affect you, your choices and actions. Know these beliefs are the reason you experience the reality you have now and seek consistently, purposefully and with unshakeable resolve to change the beliefs.

You can tackle your beliefs around money head-on with new thoughts, however, the decades of saturation throughout your psyche will have formed stains that new thoughts find challenging to scrub away.

Put money thoughts in an imaginary box. Lock it. The box is only to be opened when you have a purpose that is bigger than you and your lifetime.

Only when you are drenched in the immense vision for a greater future and the powerful, emotional drivers for making that change, will you be prepared to take down the higher-way robbing thoughts.

Keep a record of the daily flow of money in and out of your life, but do not examine the money records in detail until opening the imaginary box.

Free of money thoughts, focus on a *survival inventory*. Is there anything urgent?

Do you have everything you need to meet your and your dependants physiological and safety needs?

If not, you may need to address these as a priority above everything else.

The creditors can wait. Pay yourself first. You are setting clear boundaries for your own protection and survival. You are no use to anyone if you have a breakdown under the stress and are carried away to the debtors' prison or workhouse.

When money is out of your mind, complete a *holistic inventory*—excluding money. This is where you are now in your life.

Mind: Psychological, self-esteem, self-actualisation: examples include self-respect, knowledge and skills—mental health and well-being.

Body: Physiological and safety: examples include food, water, shelter, clothes, bed to sleep in, health essentials, safety essentials—physical health and well-being.

Heart: Social belonging, relationships: examples include family and friends, sense of community, feeling happy, nurtured and loved—emotional health and well-being.

Spirit: Self-transcendence, living ethically, legacy: examples include striving for the benefit of others or nature, investing in something bigger than yourself, seeing beyond yourself and your own needs—spiritual health and well-being.

It is easier to know the wealth you truly possess (beyond money) when working with intellectual, physical, emotional and spiritual capital. It's easier to be grateful for what you have and to know the power these capitals give you.

Next, reread your *purpose statement*.

This uses the goals you wrote down earlier.

Explore your holistic inventory in greater detail and in relation to your purpose statement.

Identify the gaps or shortfall analysis on the four capitals of physical, emotional, intellectual and spiritual. What's stopping you from achieving your goals?

Identify the actions you need to take towards your ideal life. Are you on track?

When you are ready, arrange an *imaginary box opening time*. Set aside a day. Make an appointment, which will be once a week or better still once a month. Do not enable that human invention of the mind we call *money* to destroy your one and only life, be it through chains of poverty or the noose of avarice.

Enjoy your life, allow yourself to truly live between these appointments with your money box. Spend the time between now and your first appointment focusing on the better life ahead and your remarkable purpose.

On box opening day, revisit your purpose statement, then look at your financial income and expenditure records—total them from the last box opening day.

Complete an inventory of your physical capital—what you own and what you owe.

Create totals for your expenditure by each category and sub-category.

Have the totals changed?

If so, is the movement aligned with goals?

Should you uncover an imbalance, adjust your actions for the next box opening day.

Do not give into guilt if no improvements have been made, simply restate your goals and close the box until next time. Then focus on your purpose, redouble your efforts, keep adjusting your navigation approach until you achieve the results you want.

After you have done some housekeeping on your finances you need to focus on paying down debt. Interest when added to the purchase price can often double or triple the cost of a purchase.

Save to buy.

The interest rate we pay in serving debt is usually higher than the interest we earn on our savings—the lenders take the margin as profit. So, aim to be free of unsecured debt as soon as possible. If you have insufficient income to meet minimum debt repayment levels, you may need to contact creditors to make a pro rata arrangement.

Never let this impact your self-esteem—your situation is not uncommon. Money is not your identity, so refuse to let it affect who you are.

Additionally, it is important to reduce secured debt on property and assets as soon as possible. Interest payments can triple the cost of a property purchase over the lifetime of the mortgage.

Do you hold innocent beliefs around property?

Many people believe, incorrectly, that property outperforms shares. Rental yields are lower than equity market yields when taking into account periods of tenant vacancy and all costs including maintenance, fees, taxes etc. Plus, there are liquidity issues, tax implications and the time factor of portfolio management to be considered.

Review your credit rating and seek to improve this. There are various reports available, free of charge, that demonstrate how to improve your credit history. Poor credit scores can triple the interest rates you pay on loans.

If you find your debt cannot possibly be paid in your lifetime, consider insolvency and bankruptcy as a route to wiping the slate clean. Seek guidance from your Citizens Advice Bureau.

There is no disgrace in taking this step. Thousands do it every day. You are not alone. You are not the first.

Any shame that people feel around getting support is a lie, a conditioned thought placed there by a controlling society. Financial organisations want you to spend a lifetime paying them—not having the debt wiped clear—so they massage the lie to keep you bound in debt to them.

As soon as you are able, start to create an emergency fund, the purpose of which is covering three to six months of your now reduced expenditure.

Open two bank accounts—banks tend to only make credit available to those who least need it and overcharge those who can least afford it. If a bank is being difficult with you, as they tend to do to bolster profits, you simply switch to the other account to pay bills.

When your biggest challenge is to manage from one payday to the next, as quickly as you can, get into a cycle where you are not resorting to overdrafts or payday loans. In this endeavour, timing of bill payments can be crucial to manage cash flow.

Pay at the latest opportunity given and cancel direct debits to place you in control of the timing and amounts of payments. Creditors are just helping themselves to your money in advance—the money is better sitting in your bank account, not theirs.

Do not pay others before you have paid yourself for essentials—as long as you make due payments on time, your credit rating will not be adversely affected.

Explore ways of saving money on all your purchases. When you are in debt to others, it is easy to ignore it, to bury your head in the sand, to become financially unconscious. This is not healthy!

So, remember, if you are finding it stressful, set yourself aside a money day each month when you sort your finances, this gives you four weeks every month worry free. From today, things get better.

Society has conditioned the population to consider money a taboo subject. We fear judgement on our financial decisions, yet this is another innocent belief.

Talk about money. Do not hide from it—do not lock the Hungry Ghost away… he will come back to haunt you! Fear of money is yet another attachment to material things and the GAME Plan invites you to let go of this fear.

There are worse things in life than money. And there are better things in life than money!

When a person is trapped upon the treadmill of work existence—doing a job they do not like, the question they often ask is, "How do I get off the treadmill?"

The GAME Plan of *Your Money or Your Life!* encourages you to replace the income from the job you hate with income from the job you love, supplemented with savings and investment income.

When you have built savings, you will decumulate the savings by drawing down capital, whilst at the same time making sure you do not outlive your capital.

The capital withdrawals, once built into your lifetime cash flow forecast, will ensure that you can give up the rat race at the earliest opportunity. Love the life you live, live the life you love! Sooner rather than later!

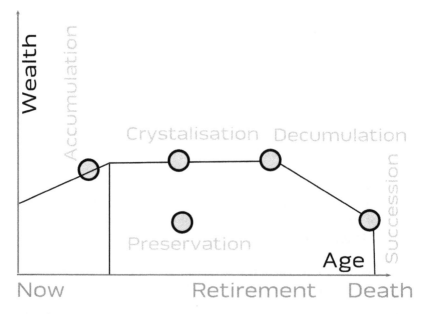

If you exceed physical capital requirements—whilst carrying deficits on the personal capitals, such as mental, emotional and spiritual—your well-being will deteriorate. Your holistic health deteriorates!

Full Wealth = Physical Capital + Mental Capital + Emotional Capital + Spiritual Capital.

When you seek to crystallise and decumulate your multifaceted resources you are enjoying the full fruits of your labour. Your inheritance to future generations is more than money, it becomes a benevolent, impactful and lasting legacy.

Your preservation and protection of *full wealth* during your lifetime is to consider and plan for your four personal tenets: body, mind, heart and spirit.

A lifetime cash flow forecast is a year-by-year forecast of your financial capital requirements designed to help you achieve your personal goals in all four tenets. You enter your multifaceted goals and financial means into a program and run various scenarios to see if you outlive your financial capital.

So long as the lifetime cash flow forecast does not go into deficit in later life, you will be surprised at how much a fall in income can be tolerated when leaving the rat race.

Consider downsizing residential property to fund higher priority needs. You could also consider working for longer before leaving the rat race or before retirement from the job you love.

Work—or shall we say economic activity to generate income—can be rewarding in not just financial ways. When you work and at the same time employ your unique skills and talents in pursuit of your life purpose (and in the creation of your lasting legacy), work no longer feels like work. It feels like a vocation.

With a lifetime cash flow forecast, a date is entered to show when the player leaves the rat race. The date can be adjusted to view the impact it has on lifetime financial capital. Usually, when leaving the rat race, income will drop in the early years. However, it could be the case that the eventual income is higher because of productivity gains from doing a job you love.

Leaving your date of escape to financial freedom longer will initially lift lifetime wealth, bringing it forward will potentially lower lifetime wealth. The aim is always to bring the desired lifestyle change sooner, rather than later.

Lowering lifetime wealth will also lower the financial legacy you leave when you are gone. However, using additional time saved from removing a long commute to focus upon a personal lasting legacy, can more than compensate for any potential loss in financial legacy.

When you escape the rat race it is not an economic loss to society—you enjoy a better quality of life; you are more usefully employed, applying skills, talents and energy creating a lasting legacy to heal the world's grief. You are likely to be more productive when inspired and your contribution to society can be even greater than before.

Another economic benefit is a potential solution to the world's widening pensions deficit from workers being willing to work longer in work they enjoy. Working into old age preserves pension pots and contributes tax revenues to support national social security.

We are retiring sooner from jobs we hate and living longer. As state pension systems are often funded by current taxpayers, a cross-subsidy exists between retired pensioners and working, younger generations. With birth rates reducing and the ratio of pensioners dependent on taxpayers increasing, the burden to fund social security is increasing for young workers.

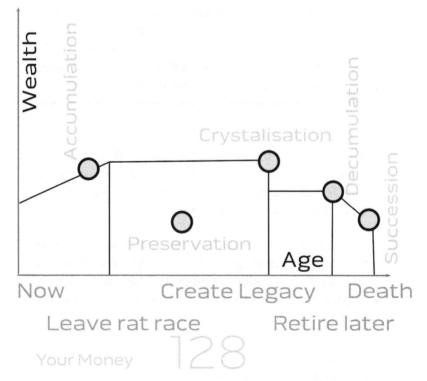

Creating your lasting legacy may require a significant financial commitment. So long as strategies can be adopted to avoid financial wealth deficit in later life, financial capital expenditure can be modelled in the lifetime cash flow forecast to accommodate this.

There are several strategies you can adopt to increase financial income. Such as earning more income in employment, gain a second employment in a job you love, shop around for better interest rates on savings, generate higher investment returns through more aggressive investment strategies, pay less tax using government incentives that improve net income, claim state benefit entitlements or rent out capital resources.

The key here is to explore all options and consider not just the money, but the *attachments* of money in the marriage of money and meaning.

The concept of money can be seen as analogous to *energy*. Energy can neither be created or destroyed, it only can be transformed through exchange from one form to another. For example, when the banks print money, this devalues the money in your pocket. When you receive a windfall, it is because of an equivalent loss elsewhere.

You are encouraged to be mindful of the damaging impact created in some forms of financial exchange. If money comes to you at the expense and disservice of others, without a fair exchange in value, this adds to world grief. This is a debit on your spiritual capital account.

If you give away money at the expense and detriment of self, without fair exchange in value, this adds to your grief. This is a debit on your physical capital account.

There is a point of balance, where a fair exchange takes place.

A person who is essentially self-enhancing will place more value on material possessions, than on emotional or spiritual values. When receiving money, they must take care to give equivalent meaning in return to the giver. When giving money, they must take care not to ask for too much meaning in return.

One who is self-transcending, will place more value on emotional and spiritual capital than money. When receiving money, they must take care not to give away too much meaning in return. When giving money, they must take care not to ask for too little meaning in return.

Ask yourself:

Does what I do harm anyone else or the planet in any way?

Am I trying to control the people and circumstances in the world?

What if everyone did this?

Be mindful of the meaning exchanged in all financial transactions and seek to do no harm. Every unit of money given is a powerful vote for the change we wish to see in the world. Spend wisely for your life purpose to make a beneficial difference in the world.

Consider the draining of natural resources from a growing world population and higher consumption demands. Humanity's consumption of natural resources outstrips Earth's production every year.

In the year 2000, all resources produced were used by October. In 2018, all resources were used by 2nd August. This trend cannot continue much longer, else we reach a tipping point.

Over-consumption depletes valuable resources and adds little to our well-being. If allowed to continue, there will come a time where we live in a world with insufficient natural resources: no food, water, shelter or clothes. At present this happens to our neighbours, one day this could happen to you or your children.

The marriage of money and meaning insists upon a responsible level of consumption; being mindful of the impacts on other people and planet. Responsible consumption levels are sustainable for the world population within the earth's annual production capacity.

All that exists in nature is sacrosanct beyond how it serves us or meets the needs of the individual self, *it is sacred!* Ask yourself, *Does my expenditure pattern add to world grief or make the world a better place?*

We live on this planet at a time of immense change—the greenhouse effect of global warming and melting polar ice caps and glaciers. Temperatures are breaking records around the world, sea levels are rising at the fastest rate in 2,000 years.

In the decade preceding 2018, over twenty million people were forcibly displaced by rising sea levels. Global flooding is set to triple in the next ten years. The problem is getting worse—Earth could warm by a further six degrees by 2100.

Imagine if you and your family were forcibly displaced by rising flood water. As seawater reaches farther inland, it can cause destructive erosion, wetland flooding, aquifer and agricultural soil contamination and lost habitat for fish, birds and plants.

Imagine if your drinking water was contaminated. Imagine the interference with farming and the damage to our economy with higher cost of water supply, inflated food prices, increased taxes to pay for costal defences, lost real estate as our coasts change.

Imagine not having clean water to drink.

Consider deforestation—destruction of rainforests and old-growth forests. Forests still cover about 30% of the world's land area, but swathes half the size of England are lost each year. The world's rain forests could completely vanish in a hundred years at the current rate of deforestation.

80% of Earth's land animals and plants live in forests and many cannot survive the deforestation that destroys their homes and turns land into desert. This results in loss of biodiversity and species extinction: between 4,000 and 6,000 species become extinct each year.

Trees are essential to life on Earth. They produce oxygen for us to breathe and absorb greenhouse gases that also cause global warming.

Consider pollution of soil, water and air, ozone layer holes, oceanic dead zones, noise pollution, radar, microwaves, radioactive contamination, thermal and light pollution. Consider sulphur dioxide and hazardous gases that cause global warming, acid rain and how their contamination of the air we breathe results in asthma and lung cancer.

Imagine reaching a tipping point where we can no longer breathe clean air. A freefall cascade in air quality, eventuating in breathable air disappearing. A runaway greenhouse effect, with people suffocating on the streets. They can't fill their lungs with air enough to make a final phone call to their loved ones. They are dying and they cannot even say goodbye.

It is easy to dismiss this scenario as science fiction, yet it undercuts everything. If we ignore this issue, this is what we are facing. And by casting the idea aside, you personally are contributing to the problem. Regardless of how widespread the tragedy is; of how you are tempted to label this as *somebody else's problem*, you are accountable. You must ask yourself, *Do you trust governments and banks to create change?*

Almost 60% of Earth's species live in water. Industrial waste is dumped into our rivers and oceans leading to severe contamination and death of species. Pesticides spoil our ground water systems; oil spills pollute our water supplies. Detergents block sunlight, make water uninhabitable, contaminate our food chain and increases epidemic diseases such as cholera and diarrhoea.

Imagine having nothing to eat, no clean water to drink and the doctor diagnosing you with a terminal illness, giving you only a few months to live!

Consider nuclear plant malfunctions and improper nuclear waste disposal, causing cancer, blindness, infertility, birth defects and the poisoning of our soil, air and water. Imagine if you or a close family member were diagnosed with cancer and had lost your sight as a result of losing a geographic lottery.

Imagine if you or your loved ones were diagnosed with a deadly flu strain. What if you only had days to live?

What did you not get to do?

What would you regret?

As you look over your life would you say you had lived well?

Would you have a good death?

Would you have created your lasting legacy?

Consider superintelligence not obeying moral rules.

Those risks include extreme wealth inequality in the future, a major bioengineering accident or a potentially species-ending disaster. AI (artificial intelligence) computers already have the ability to develop their own languages, yet our response is to believe a species-ending disaster will never happen.

We say credit card debt is a frightening reality and forget that arrangements with creditors need not be life threatening. We are terrified by debt, but superintelligence is a very real threat. There are possibilities that we simply cannot ignore. What if you were to pay no attention to them?

Consider nanotechnology, smart poison and gnatbots. Ponder nanotechnology's impact on society, on human health and the environment, on trade, on security, on food systems.

When the developers of this technology come from a place of self-enhancing values, it is terrifying. It is equally inspiring as developers embrace self-transcending values for the benefit of people and planet. Where better that we see a move from imbalance to balance than in our industries?

The earth provides food, shelter, clothing, warmth from fuel sources, water to drink and bathe, flowers, trees, beauty and the air we breathe. The earth sustains and enhances our physical life.

People often divorce themselves from their planet. They view the earth as something *other* than themselves, as if they are one thing and the earth is something else—something *less than*. Everything you are, comes from and is, the earth!

Pollution in the ocean is pollution in your bloodstream. Toxins in the atmosphere are toxins in your lungs—and bloodstream. Chemicals in the soil are chemicals in your flesh. When you die, you do not go back to the earth, you never stopped being the earth!

In Bolivia, the earth was given legal rights in 2010. The law established the juridical character of the earth as *"collective subject of public interest,"* to ensure the exercise and protection of Earth's rights. By giving the earth a legal personality, Earth can, through specific representatives (humans), bring an action to defend its rights.

Consider how you spend money.

Every pound, dollar, euro, yen we spend is a powerful vote for the change we want to see in the world. Investments are also a very powerful tool for being the change you want to see in the world. If everyone invested their life savings in accordance with their values the world could know a reality that currently does not exist in the physical world.

It is easy to select sustainable, responsible investments—these days the choice is wide and need not be at the expense of lower investment returns. There is an information imbalance in the investment industry, so be mindful of where fair exchange exists and where it does not.

When investing with a self-enhancing investment manager, you must be aware the manager may overstate the value given and understate the price taken. This may cause suffering, even if the investment manager acts in ignorance and believes a fair exchange was made.

The intellectual investment manager has a strong technical understanding of money but may have little comprehension of emotions or spirituality (doing the right thing). As such, you risk losing money, because the manager adds little personal value in the exchange of the price charged for his or her services.

For example, active fund managers may claim that they can beat the market by timing the markets and choosing stocks, when in reality 90% of stock returns are determined by the initial asset allocation made. Timing and stock selection add little value and add a great deal of cost.

An investment manager can charge three times the cost of buying a market index tracking fund and 99% of the time[9] fails to deliver more than the market, after charges are taken, over the long term.

When you have the funds to invest, following the GAME plan of *Your Money or Your Life!* you will discover there are several more steps you can also take to invest wisely. This is the next step, *Execution*.

EXECUTION

When it comes to execution, you implement your financial plan by manifesting the changes you want to see in your life and your finances—your financial decisions. There is an ongoing review process where you recreate purpose statements for subsequent cycles from creation to manifestation.

Many people fail to execute or, worse still, only partially execute.

Failing to execute results in unfulfilled dreams and lifetime regrets, whilst partial execution could see you give up financial security and fail to implement necessary income generation solutions.

The Execution phase transports you to a sense of greater empowerment. It enables you to gain sovereignty over your thoughts and life, connect with your intuition, emotions and instinct. Your goal is to live well, sustainably in accordance with your values and using your power to create a lasting legacy in the world, to heal your part of world grief. Your aim is to walk the higher way.

At the Execution stage, check to see if anything has changed for you since Means. If anything urgent has cropped up, you may deal with it or park it for later.

Most people have a great deal to gain from moving from imbalance to balance, by playing the game. You do have the power and ability to break free of your feeling of inertia—to become financially free—where that tipping point means you can live the life you love. You hold the dice. You can roll the dice.

As you are aiming for the shortest trajectory to reach your goal, your personal GAME Plan must be efficient or else it needs adjustment. Should you drift off the path of purpose, the world will usually remind you with a sharp prod in the ribs. You need to be aware of this and make corrections.

Schedule a series of check-ins and follow ups, to ensure you do what you say you are going to do. It is useful to enter into an accountability agreement with a friend, to remind you and encourage you along the way. Appoint your accountability partner and share your plan with them.

You are bound to encounter resistance at some point, for every action there is a reaction—you are all but guaranteed to encounter a higher-way robber. Although, based on your Action session, you are now well equipped to overcome obstacles.

You will happen upon new challenges, resources, possibilities and opportunities. You may even need to go back and revisit earlier stages of the GAME Plan—it is a living document requiring ongoing attention and revision.

Whatever the scenario you are faced with, run a multi-capital inventory. If you *go back three spaces* take your mind out of the money and think mind, body, heart and spirit.

Use the elemental system. Let go of innocent beliefs you hold around money. Deal with anything urgent and life threatening, then start to build. Do not lose sight of your end game. A life well lived and a lasting legacy aligned with your values is still on the table, and achievable once you recover financially.

When you get paid, emotionally it feels good—you get excited at the possibilities of what you can buy. Before you do anything, check your multifaceted needs of the four tenets. Make sure your decision to spend is aligned with who you want to be in the world. Bring your thought process back to the GAME Plan.

If you get an opportunity to buy property, you may get excited. Before you do anything, check your multifaceted needs. Does buying the property serve your greater purpose of who you want to be in the world. Or, is it just your ego talking? Make your decisions based on ticking all the boxes that enrich a purposeful life.

When you are given money, you enter a pit of pleasure emotionally. Check again with the GAME Plan. Where did the money come from, did it harm anyone, did it cause destruction to the planet? Or, does it carry a value that gives you credit across all four capitals?

If you want to invest it, think about how you invest it. If you want to spend it, think about how you want to spend it. You may simply want to do nothing, if it serves who you want to be in the world then that's fine too.

Know your purpose and values. When you have a clear ethos, you will consider how your life translates into the four capitals and what actions you need to take. What you do instinctively, rationally and emotionally and whether these fit with what you intuitively know to be your values-driven path.

What do you need to do as a result?

What behavioural corrections do you need to make to ensure that change happens?

In life, you are taught by society a set of behaviours that you *should* do. Now you are equipped to question these teachings. You know to check if the lessons are coming from a place of imbalance that will drive you off course or if they come from a place of greater balance that will drive you towards your goals.

In life, you are bombarded by the law, the Government and media, telling you what the most important things in life are. Now you are equipped to sense check the instruction against your mind, body, heart, spirit agenda.

Not all authoritative instructions come from a place of balance in the world. You can filter these instructions. You can create your own rules.

In life, authorities might tell you that money is important—they leverage your need for food, housing and relationships. They tie the instruction to all the things you hold dear and precious to make you frightened. Your physical, mental, emotional and spiritual goals also tie into these things—a decision just based on money has the potential to destroy the things you hold most dearly.

Those who seek to influence you will always tie in what they want with the benefits of those things you fundamentally connect to as essential. You now have a mind, body, heart and spirit filter to sense check those influences against.

When you believe money impacts your security, food on the table, your home and supporting your family, bankruptcy can be terrifying.

The truth is, a bankruptcy still leaves us secure, with food on the table, a roof above our heads and support for our family. Whereas, compromising your values can be gut-wrenching and cause reactions and consequences that impact these things far more severely. They can kill you!

Yes, mind, body, heart and spirit deficits kill people. People attempt suicide because they are depressed, are suffering mental health issues, impulsive, crying out for help, philosophically desire to die or they make a mistake. They may have a pervasive sense of suffering as well as the belief that escape is hopeless.

When you seek to manifest abundance, do not think just financial capital. Excess financial capital is proven to reduce well-being. Ask yourself what decisions you must take to move you towards your balanced life, in equilibrium, well-lived and your lasting legacy.

Execution can be made as easy as online banking by using a platform.

Make use of savings accounts for the emergency funds you may need to access in the short term: three to six months. They are unsuitable for long-term savers—five years plus—due to the relatively low returns when compared to conventional investments.

The income lost could instead be usefully employed in delivering you to an earlier financial freedom and then funding a life well lived, an ethical life and your lasting legacy.

There is no such thing as a *low-risk investment with high expected returns*. If it sounds too good to be true it probably is. There are no crystal balls, so, if the manager claims they can time markets or pick stocks to beat markets and justify their high fees—run!

If you hear that everyone is buying a stock or some amazing opportunity, you are already too late to buy. The price is already high. If word comes through to you that everyone is selling a stock or opportunity, you are already too late to sell. The price is already low.

Avoid buying high and selling low! Buy and hold, in the cycle of the markets lows become highs in time and vice versa. Buy when you need to buy and sell when you need to sell.

Diversify. Buy globally diversified funds, not individual stocks and securities—you want to avoid holding all your eggs in one basket.

Only invest in what you understand. If it is a *boring* fund, that's a good sign as many a litigation lawyer can tell you. Only buy regulated investments, as the regulator has done much of the checking for you. You are protected by the regulation and compensation schemes should things go wrong.

The only certainty when investing is cost—always keep costs low. Use passive instruments such as market trackers where possible, in the long run few managers beat the markets after charges. There are plenty of sustainable, responsible index tracker funds to choose from.

Investing is easier than you think—online platforms are as simple as online bank accounts. You do not need the person in the middle; you need the cost of middle-people less. 95% do not have access to middle-people anyway. You can go online and buy tax-efficient, ethical, low-cost, regulated investments direct.

Ethically filter your asset selection according to your beliefs and values—follow your purpose. Each fund is rated with an ESG rating (Environmental Social Governance). Three stars and above is a good rating.

Allocate your assets according to your risk appetite and capacity for loss. A good starting point is to take your age from 100, this gives you the proportion of your portfolio to be held in equities.

For example, if I was aged 60 I would hold 40% of my portfolio in equities. It goes down as you get older as you have less time to recover losses. Adjust according to your capacity for loss, that is your answer to the question if I lost all of this could I still live comfortably. If the answer is no, dial down the risk by reducing your equity holding.

For ordinary people with low savings levels, try to pay down your debt as quickly as you can. Keep a check on your credit score. Aim to be neither a borrower or a lender at your earliest opportunity. Lenders prefer to only lend to borrowers who do not really need the money and reflect this in the pricing.

In the absence of a lifetime cash flow forecasting tool or spreadsheets, this is a simple way to budget to ensure you do not outlive your capital. If you were to invest your portfolio in a blend of 60% equities and 40% fixed-interest securities (bonds) and draw down 4% of your portfolio in cash annually, then in the long run the capital value of your portfolio is expected to be preserved in real terms.

That is, even after considering inflation, the value when you sell will be preserved, about the same value as when you bought. Clearly, markets go up and down and the value you take out may be less than the value you paid in. But the expectation under the rule of 4% is that these values will be about the same.

For instance, if you have sold your house and have £100,000 to invest, you can draw down £4,000 per annum and still have that deposit of £100,000 to put down as a deposit on your next purchase.

An example of this could be if you wanted a retirement income of £40,000 you would need to save a pension pot of £1,000,000. If you take more than 4%, the *safe withdrawal rate*, you erode the underlying capital.

If you invest, expecting a return after inflation of 4%, your capital can be expected to double after eighteen years. The aim might to be to skid in on the last day on your deathbed with £1 in the bank, saying "boy what a great life!" Who knows?

It is *your* life plan.

PART FIVE
YOUR MONEY OR YOUR LIFE

1904, Brentwood in Maryland, USA. Elizabeth Magie was a 38-year-old writer, actress and feminist, whose friends called her Lizzie. Lizzie was values based, whole and balanced—she chose to live each day according to her values, with a balance of meaning and money.

During the summer months, she visited the newly founded community in Arden in Delaware, to test a board game she was developing. Residents in Arden led a simple life during the summer months, living in tents and rustic homes. Arden's people encouraged artistic and intellectual expression, through which grew the deep sense of community.

Lizzie loved it there.

Arden was a single-tax community, which is an economic philosophy where value derived from land, such as land taxes, should be distributed to the community by way of a citizen's dividend. Land in Arden could not be sold, instead it had a renewable 99-year lease. The leasehold interest in the land had a market value and could be sold.

The political goal of single tax was to raise public revenue, mainly from a land value tax paid by the landowners. It was intended to reduce economic inequality, increase economic efficiency, remove incentives to under-utilise urban land and reduce property speculation.

Lizzie wanted to teach children about economic imbalance, hoping that, playing the game, would provoke their suspicion of unfairness in property speculation. She wanted the kids to know how the rents on property enriched property owners and impoverished tenants. She hoped that the kids might carry this knowledge into their adulthood.

Lizzie called her game the *Landlord's Game*.

It was a bit of a failure, as people found it too complicated. Lizzie had never patented the game, so there was nothing she could do when college students encountered her game and started to make up their own versions.

Versions of Lizzie's creation started to appear all over the place under a variety of names, such as, *Finance*, *Auction* and eventually *Monopoly*.

As is often the case in the history of economics the meaning of the game was soon lost in the evolution of the different commercial iterations. Lizzie's altruistic purpose was forgotten as greed took over and the game became just about the money. It developed into a money-making game, where the object was to bankrupt your opponents.

In honour of Lizzie, inadvertent originator of the world's bestselling board game, we can use a board game format to develop a personalised strategy for success. As now apparent, this game is called *Your Money or Your Life!* and, as the name suggests, it seeks to restore the balance between meaning and money in your life.

Starting with the GAME Plan, playing the game moves you from imbalance to balance. It teaches you that *rich* can be what you hold in your heart, as well as your bank account. If we are living our life purpose and building our lasting legacy, we can live responsibly and enjoy lasting contentment. We can live with a healthy balance between wealth and well-being.

Living life dictated by the current banking ethos ensures people are controlled by their money, rather than take control of it. They are a token on the board rather than the player of the game. They are moved by someone else's dice throw. As a result, they either have money and little life or they have life and little money.

When you examine today's financial system, it is reminiscent of daylight robbery or rather *highway robbery*. Life robs you—it robs you of your money and most importantly, it robs you of your birthright: abundance in every aspect of the four tenets.

Banks cannot be trusted as they serve the financial elite, as a method of serving themselves. Banks manipulate you into chasing money, living a wage-slavery life in this endeavour. And, while on the work treadmill, we run faster and harder, in fear of not surviving.

The truth is, money and life are inextricably linked. There is a form or shape to money and life for you.

Even in extreme cases we witness a relationship between life and money. When facing utter poverty, money can mean the difference between life and death. Those with profound wealth soon discover there is no such thing as all work and no play. In life, there is a seed of money. In money, there is a seed of life.

Money and life must always exist in harmony when we seek lasting contentment. This harmony disappears when imbalance of any kind is created, because imbalance causes the situation to disintegrate—to take on another form or shape.

The balance between life and money is in a constant state of flux, running in a cycle, each attempting to gain dominance over the other depending on the time and circumstances. When one achieves dominance over the other, an imbalance occurs causing suffering. The influence of the dominant aspect subsides and the other takes over.

These are the ups and downs of daily existence. Good luck and bad luck. Growth and decay. Life and death.

Your Money or Your Life! introduces you to how you can maintain a perfect balance of money and life. Accept with equanimity where there is imbalance and where there is imbalance, start again. There's never a permanent end to this journey.

Nothing stays permanent.

All phenomena are a series of cyclic patterns in one endless cycle of change. Perceive, contemplate and be mindful of the grand and ongoing nature of transformation.

Your higher way is attained when you marry life and money. Like any virtuous and long-lasting marriage there are strains and tensions in the relationship which can create imbalance to be tolerated and then corrected. Harmony requires constant awareness, increasingly profound realisation of our true nature, intuitive insight, sensitivity and constant corrective action.

The result is a life-changing sense of contentment, a deepening wisdom and joy with your world. The side effects are youthful invigoration, excellent health and physical vigour, and a long and happy life.

When the higher way is achieved you never feel bored or frustrated, you never react in detrimental ways to loss, bereavement, anxiety or fear. You become an agreeable person as you manifest a core sense of inner happiness.

The higher way requires wisdom: higher thought. Wisdom combines intellect, intuition, feelings, and instinct. Through wisdom our relationship with life and money improves.

If you are clever with money you can improve every aspect of your life. You can preserve your wealth. You can command a life lived in harmony with yourself, other people and the world. You can do what you love all the time, with even work becoming something you adore.

If a person is not so clever with money, they can ruin every aspect of their life. Their life can be in disorder and tension, as they become more and more miserable. Their actions can be harmful to themselves, other people and the planet. They constantly find displeasure in what they do—their life is merely a treadmill of fear and work existence.

If you are clever with your life, you can improve your finances. You can make conscious lifestyle choices that align your income, savings and expenditure with what you love and believe.

When a person is not so clever with life, they struggle to make ends meet, proceeding blindly without awareness of the financial consequences of their actions, money ends up eluding you.

We can be clever. We can use our money wisely. We can earn wisely. We can give less of our life in exchange for money if we leverage a useful gift or talent.

Thus far in your life's journey, you have a deep sense of holding back; that you have something very special to share with the world. You have a useful gift or talent, which in the offering awakens something within you, giving your life meaning and purpose.

Invest your time and gifts wisely to make money. Invest your money wisely to make time— time for the good things in life. Over the course of this book, you have uncovered the secrets to a life-changing journey—the journey of how to invest yourself into a magnificent quest.

The aim of *Your Money or Your Life!* is to build a lasting legacy. The focus is not about the money, although if your money runs out it will end the game for you. The game is about using your money to create a meaningful life—walking the middle path of balancing intuition, emotion, instinct and intellect in your life

The board of *Your Money or Your Life!* is a navigational aid: a compass that orientates us on the map of life and enables us through the roll the dice. As we play, we learn how to navigate the lower way, whilst remaining upon the higher way—with the long-term aim of changing the world towards a higher way.

As you cycle around the board, you develop your life plan. Initially through the GAME Plan, but as you evolve your strategy, you bring more and more elements into play. Eventually you can play the game with others, understanding how we can interact with other people and the world, through The High Way experience.

Having completed your GAME Plan, I recommend progressing to the workbook, which accompanies this book—*Stand and Deliver! Discovering Your Money and Your Life.*

How you play the game demonstrates how you are living your life—with volition or without, by design or by default. This appreciation for how your actions, behaviours, choices and beliefs affect results, will highlight your position as disintermediated, underserved or served.

Armed with this knowledge you can set about changing how well you are served, in all four tenets of your life. Through employing profound values, using your spending votes and developing a lasting legacy, you live through depth of ideals, breadth of scope and longevity of action.

The game takes you through the cycle of life, from birth to death and how the five elements—accumulation, crystallisation, decumulation, succession and preservation— aid you throughout your life.

The workbook will also help you take your existing GAME Plan and enhance it with further questions, activities and gaming strategies. Developing and evolving a detailed and comprehensive life plan, needs to be instilled in the creation, with the same sense of fun as you want your life to contain.

From the understanding of big-picture goals, to a range of actions, transactional and financial details of the means, to systemic and planned execution, life is enormous; beyond our comprehension. Yet, it is lived in the tiniest of moments: the little things that merge into one another to guide us from birth to grave.

Whilst you believe what banks, the Government and the media want you to believe, life is not fun—it is not a game to be enjoyed. The moment you rewrite the rules and nurturing all four capitals, you transcend the toil of the lower way and start navigating from a higher way.

You discover how to notice, avoid and deal with the higher-way robbers, who seek to bring you down, steal from you and leave you for dead. You learn how a one-size-fits-all plan will never truly fulfil you or your needs, desires and dreams.

The challenge when stepping onto the higher way, is in the current reality, we cannot give up the lower way completely. We are bound by bank accounts, investments, money and the veil of lies that surround these. To ignore them is to lose touch with the *real world*.

The world of finance can be terrifying as we venture into it. It feels like a minefield as we place our every step. Let's not forget, the financial industry is here to serve you. It is unavoidable.

The financial industry performs essential functions such as enabling savings and investments, providing protection from risks and supporting the growth of industries. There's no path around the minefield. It's just a natural part of your everyday life.

Experiences of recent years have revealed a range of vulnerabilities in the money industry. Critiques include the sector being unstable, parasitic and extractive. These issues have proved extremely costly for society and resulted in a significant loss of public trust and confidence.

However, life planning is just the beginning when it comes to changing this for the better—and the betterment of all. As you start to walk the higher way, investing in all four capitals and becoming literate in the languages of each, you will begin to knock the legs out of the corrupt establishment.

Initially, when confronting the time-kilned behemoth—the banking industry—you may feel alone in your endeavours. Yet, as you continue to live the life of your dreams, others will notice and join you. Together, our unified voice will demand ethical business, conscious investments and a shifting from narrow financial wealth to holistic wealth.

Much soul-searching has been necessary as we cycle from one economic crisis to another. However, this has largely been technical or quantitative in nature through surveillance and regulation. Ethical and behavioural aspects of risk-management failures are still comparatively neglected. When people use their power, then ethics and behaviour will change in organisations.

Performance incentive schemes will be redesigned, and the interests of all stakeholders will be better represented. Shareholder value, client satisfaction and general citizenship will be included in performance targets. All organisations will become values based and focus on a quadruple bottom line for Profit, People, Planet and Purpose.

There will be checks made on the movement of ministers, regulators and corporate leaders into the offices of each other. In a transparent society, status positions cannot be granted as rewards for past deeds. We will monitor revolving doors and filter for imbalance.

We will remove corruption from all institutions big and small with fit and proper assessments to include *values* vetting in the industry, just as we vet credit history.

There will be a time when everyone is inherently values based. The shadow of misinformation has been the only obstacle to reformation. As we eagerly embrace change once the truth becomes clear, we will rehabilitate imbalanced leaders, lifting fingers from their death grip on leadership positions and encourage the development of balanced leadership.

Universal *codes of conduct* will be introduced, to raise levels of ethical action and professionalism. These will be values based, not rules based. And they will be enforced.

Whistle-blowers will be protected and oaths will be taken by leaders who promise to represent the best interests of all stakeholders. Fiduciary standards will be introduced to remove all conflicts of interest.

Businesses do not change while their profits are good. As soon as enough people create a tipping point that damages the income of a business, they listen. And when the voice they hear, en masse, is repeating the absolute need for trust, altruism and compassion, they will change (and be more successful because of that change).

We will encourage balanced leadership in industry and within the regulators. Organisations will have *values* directors, rather than compliance directors. This is not so much about de-risking and sustaining institutions with a culture of imbalance, it is about significant corporate-cultural overhaul for balance, a greater contribution to world peace and saving the planet.

Where market participants are currently adopting imbalanced characteristics, with a "let the buyer beware" approach, overly complex products and services will carry Government Wealth Warnings: *"Buyer Beware!"*

Product advertising will be values-censured, with imbalanced marketing spending curtailed. The financial industry will be akin to the tobacco industry, with the dominant sales and marketing apparatus of product or service-oriented companies dismantled.

This will apply equally across all distribution channels. For ordinary people who are disintermediated, orphaned and underserved (by the imbalanced intermediating community), product-selling apparatus will not convert to imbalanced call centres. This simply locks citizens in to unsuitable arrangements.

Instead, people of all levels of abundance, from all walks of life, will have access to balanced financial guidance and education programmes. They will be given the freedom to live the lives that they choose to live and not as product and service providers expect them to live.

This is no small feat for us—we are as addicted to the system as everybody else. Just as Alcoholics Anonymous supports those recovering from substance abuse and Weight Watchers helps people to create healthier eating strategies, *Your Money or Your Life!* is a detox from money addiction.

It will emancipate you from wage slavery and the prison that currently exists when it comes to the financial industry stranglehold upon us. And, as with any road to recovery and sobriety, having people around you, to walk with you and offer mutual support is always important.

A career built in the banking world enabled me to help millions through ethical banking products—whilst achieving profits through respect of people, purpose and planet. It is now my mission to help others climb onto that higher way of living.

As a pioneer on this journey, I am immensely grateful to you and welcome you to join me on the next chapter of this adventure. For as banks and their corporate brethren block your path and demand you "Stand and deliver," the game awaits…

And it is time for you to discover *Your Money AND Your Life!*

Notes

1 One of the world's largest PR companies, Edelman
2 Standard Life YouGov Survey
3 US Trust Bank of America
4 http://ptgmedia.pearsoncmg.com/images/9780133382594/sam-plepages/0133382591.pdf
5 Financial Lives Survey, Financial Conduct Authority, UK, October 2017.
6 Money Advice Service [MAS], 2013
7 World Happiness Survey https://s3.amazonaws.com/happiness-report/2018/ES-WHR.pdf
8 New Evidence on Mutal Fund Performance: A Comparison of Alternative Bootstrap Methods, David Blake et al, Journal of Financial and Quantitative Analysis, Volume 52 Issue 3, 2017
9 Perceptions Matter: The Common Cause UK Values Survey 2016. www.commoncausefoundation.org

ACKNOWLEDGEMENTS

My Dad, James Henry Conley, who inspired my outer successes and my Mum, Sylvia Morrison-Bird, who inspired my internal journey and who remains my greatest fan.

Mister Lazelle, my Art teacher at Cheadle Hulme High School, who taught me that art contributes as much to society as science and gave me my first public speaking role in the school debating society.

Terry Black, sales director at Refuge Assurance who gave me my first role in financial marketing.

Hugo Thorman, marketing director at Abbey National, who gave me my first break in the banks.

My good friend, George Kinder, founder of the global life-planning movement, who taught me everything I needed to know about life planning.

Andy Agathangelou for his inspiring leadership of the Transparency Taskforce: a collaborative community of like-minded individuals seeking to restore trust and confidence in the global financial industry.

Andy Harrington, the maker of many a professional speaker.

Richard Hagen, inspired publisher extraordinaire.

And Martyn Pentecost, amazing author and coach, who shaped a six-inch pile of ideas into a publication I can take pride in.

STEVE CONLEY

Your story is the heart of this book. Your journey from debt or despair to freedom in all areas of your life.

A few years ago, I appeared to have it all, yet my own journey made me realise that there was so much more...

I had climbed the corporate ladder of success in banking to the very top, where I headed investments for a few of the world's largest banks. I chaired industry committees, advised Parliament, led markets, won awards. Eight out of ten investors now use my products. According to the World Health Organisation, one of my products even helped save the lives of five million children.

But this didn't really matter to those who hold the keys to the vaults. They don't care that they are the least-trusted industry on the planet. But I did, and I do!

As my fellow bankers slathered greedily at the prospect of building a debt mountain by handing down sentences to wage slavery, I held the keys to freedom. I vowed to use those keys.

Ever since, I have used those keys as a life and money coach, on a mission to free millions of lost souls from the shackles forced on them by the banks.

Now I get to use those keys by delivering the secrets that the banks don't want me to share to people like you around the globe.

And of course, I enjoy my own personal financial freedom. Doing what I love. In a place I love. With people I love.

If you are ready now to plan your escape to your own financial freedom, you already know who to contact. Everything you need is below. Let's meet up and write the next chapter of your story.

STEVE@AOLP.CO.UK

HTTPS://WWW.FACEBOOK.COM/BORNTOBETHECHANGE

ONLINE COURSES AND EVENTS
HTTPS://WWW.ACADEMYOFLIFEPLANNING.COM/

MPOWR TITLES

WHEN FISH CLIMB TREES

Mel Loizou
ISBN—978-1-907282-85-0
*For those who are fed up of quick-fix solutions in the workplace
and who want rich, productive relationships and results which
flow from affirming values.*

SPEAK PERFORMANCE

Ges Ray
ISBN—978-1-907282-87-4
*For those afraid of speaking in front of a small team, groups of
strangers or large crowds. How to be a confident, compelling
and convincing speaker.*

X CHANGE

Lucia Kinght
ISBN—978-1-907282-90-4
*For those who are ready to torch their work treadmill, retire
their boss, dump the ingrates, torment the passive-aggressives,
escape the toxic office, get their fierce on and design the career
that lets them live, love and laugh after 40.*

THE KEY: TO BUSINESS AND PERSONAL SUCCESS

Martyn Pentecost
ISBN—978-1-907282-17-1
For those who are passionate about growing and developing. How to discover yourself and the most effective ways for you to flourish and enjoy success.

WRITE YOUR BOOK, GROW YOUR BUSINESS

Richard Hagen
ISBN—978-1-907282-54-6
For consultants, trainers, entrepreneurs and busines experts who want to write a book to grow your business. How to avoid the most dangerous pitfalls and set yourself up for maximum succcess before you start to write.

YOUR SLIDES SUCK!

David Henson
ISBN—978-1-907282-78-2
For all speakers who need to show information visually. How to make engaging, empowering and effective PowerPoint presentations.

LEGACY

Martyn Pentecost
ISBN: 978-1-907282-48-5
For those who wish to achieve immortality by leaving a profound legacy. Uncover the nature of lasting legacy and forge your mark through relationships, creativity, family and your work or business.

Lightning Source UK Ltd.
Milton Keynes UK
UKHW020959201022
410800UK00016B/1049

9 781907 282775